plurall

Parabéns!
Agora você faz parte do **Plurall**, a plataforma digital do seu livro didático! Acesse e conheça todos os recursos e funcionalidades disponíveis para as suas aulas digitais.

Baixe o aplicativo do **Plurall** para Android e IOS ou acesse www.plurall.net e cadastre-se utilizando o seu código de acesso exclusivo:

AAAFD4TTQ

Este é o seu código de acesso Plurall. Cadastre-se e ative-o para ter acesso aos conteúdos relacionados a esta obra.

@plurallnet
@plurallnetoficial

SOMOS EDUCAÇÃO

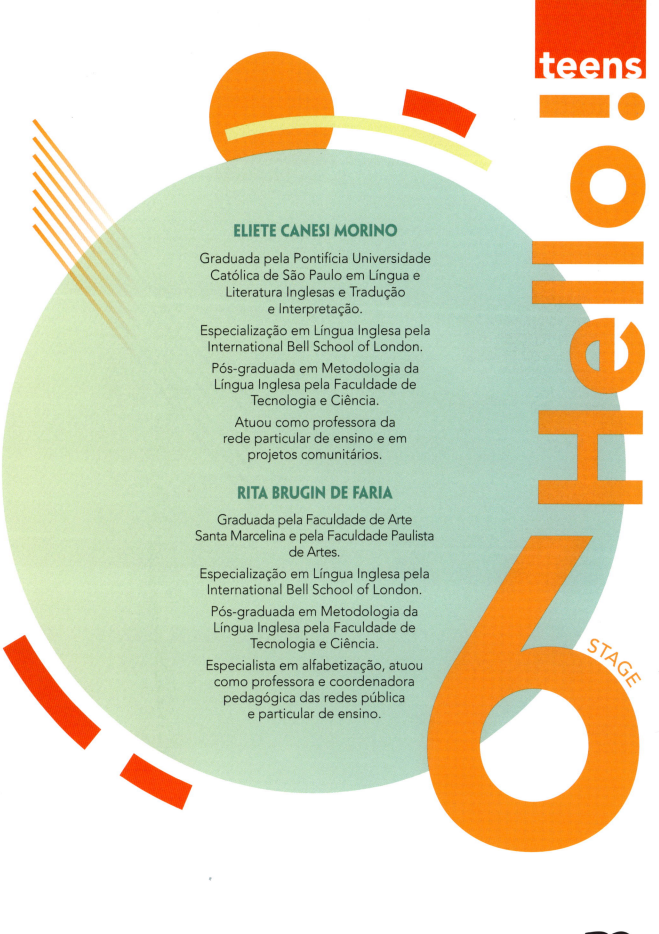

Direção Presidência: Mario Ghio Júnior
Direção de Conteúdo e Operações: Wilson Troque
Direção editorial: Luiz Tonolli e Lidiane Vivaldini Olo
Gestão de projeto editorial: Mirian Senra
Gestão de área: Alice Silvestre
Coordenação: Renato Malkov
Edição: Ana Lucia Militello, Carla Fernanda Nascimento (assist.), Caroline Santos, Danuza Dias Gonçalves, Maiza Prande Bernardello, Milena Rocha (assist.), Sabrina Cairo Bileski
Planejamento e controle de produção: Patrícia Eiras e Adjane Queiroz
Revisão: Hélia de Jesus Gonsaga (ger.), Kátia Scaff Marques (coord.), Rosângela Muricy (coord.), Ana Curci, Ana Paula C. Malfa, Arali Gomes, Brenda T. M. Morais, Diego Carbone, Gabriela M. Andrade, Luciana B. Azevedo, Luís M. Boa Nova, Patricia Cordeiro, Paula Rubia Baltazar; Amanda T. Silva e Bárbara de M. Genereze (estagiárias)
Arte: Daniela Amaral (ger.), Catherine Saori Ishihara (coord.) e Letícia Lavôr (edit. arte)
Diagramação: Estúdio Lima
Iconografia e tratamento de imagem: Sílvio Kligin (ger.), Claudia Bertolazzi (coord.), Carlos Luvizari (pesquisa iconográfica), Cesar Wolf e Fernanda Crevin (tratamento)
Licenciamento de conteúdos de terceiros: Thiago Fontana (coord.), Flavia Zambon e Angra Marques (licenciamento de textos), Erika Ramires, Luciana Pedrosa Bierbauer, Luciana Cardoso Sousa e Claudia Rodrigues (analistas adm.)
Ilustrações: Fido Nesti, Filipe Rocha, Nik Neves, Olavo Costa e Ricardo J. Souza
Cartografia: Eric Fuzii (coord.), Robson Rosendo da Rocha (edit. arte)
Design: Gláucia Koller (ger.), Talita Guedes (proj. gráfico e capa) e Gustavo Vanini (assist. arte)
Foto de capa: Kevin Dodge/Corbis/Getty Images

Todos os direitos reservados por Editora Ática S.A.
Avenida das Nações Unidas, 7221, 3º andar, Setor A
Pinheiros – São Paulo – SP – CEP 05425-902
Tel.: 4003-3061
www.atica.com.br / editora@atica.com.br

Dados Internacionais de Catalogação na Publicação (CIP)

```
Morino, Eliete Canesi
    Hello teens 6º ano / Eliete Canesi Morino, Rita Brugin
de Faria. - 8. ed. - São Paulo : Ática, 2019.

    Suplementado pelo manual do professor.
    Bibliografia.
    ISBN: 978-85-08-19332-5 (aluno)
    ISBN: 978-85-08-19333-2 (professor)

    1.   Língua inglesa (Ensino fundamental). I. Faria,
Rita Brugin de. II. Título.

2019-0112                                    CDD: 372.652
```

Julia do Nascimento - Bibliotecária - CRB-8/010142

2023
Código da obra CL 742202
CAE 648308 (AL) / 648309 (PR)
8ª edição
5ª impressão
De acordo com a BNCC.

Impressão e acabamento: EGB Editora Gráfica Bernardi Ltda.

Uma publicação SOMOS EDUCAÇÃO

WELCOME, STUDENTS, TO HELLO! TEENS 6

Hello!

A língua inglesa está cada vez mais presente no nosso dia a dia. Ela chega até nós por intermédio dos mais diversos canais de comunicação e, assim, a todo momento estamos ouvindo, lendo e falando espontaneamente em inglês.

Em virtude da evolução da tecnologia, as distâncias tornaram-se virtuais e o inglês é o idioma mais utilizado por pessoas de diferentes nacionalidades que querem se comunicar entre si.

A **Coleção Hello! Teens**, escrita para você, um adolescente do mundo contemporâneo, quer motivá-lo a aprender inglês por meio de temas instigantes associados a atividades que facilitarão sua aprendizagem.

Participe ativamente das aulas refletindo e interagindo com seus colegas e desfrute de todos os benefícios que esta aprendizagem pode lhe proporcionar!

As autoras

CONTENTS

	WORD WORK	FOCUS ON LANGUAGE	LISTEN AND SPEAK	READ AND WRITE	TIPS FOR LIFE
WELCOME! P. 6	Polite words, the alphabet, numbers 1 to 100, days of the week and months, school objects and classroom commands				
UNIT 1 A Global World P. 10	Countries and nationalities	Subject pronouns, verb to be (affirmative, long and short forms)	Greetings, introductions and nationalities	E-pals chat / Personal introduction	Respect diversity
UNIT 2 Who Is This Family? P. 24	Family members	Subject pronouns, possessive adjectives, genitive case ('), verb to be (affirmative and negative, long and short forms), short answers	Namazzi's family description / Family tree presentation	Personal profile / Family presentation	Love and respect your family!
REVIEW	Units 1 and 2 - p. 38 and 39				
UNIT 3 Home Sweet Home P. 40	Different types of houses, parts of a house and furnishings	There to be (all forms), short answers	House description and address / Present a dream house	On-line ad for rent / Produce an ad to rent or sell a dream house	Cooperation: helping with the house chores
UNIT 4 Getting Around Town P. 54	Places in town	Preposition of place, imperative (affirmative, negative)	Ask and give directions / Draw a map and give directions	Infographic about safety / Create an infographic	Beware on the streets
REVIEW	Units 3 and 4 - p. 68 and 69				

4 FOUR

	WORD WORK	FOCUS ON LANGUAGE	LISTEN AND SPEAK	READ AND WRITE	TIPS FOR LIFE
UNIT 5 Animal World P. 70	Different animals	Adjectives, indefinite articles (a/an), can (ability, all forms)	Animals can… Describe animals	Fact files about animals Produce an animal fact file	Respect and care for animals
UNIT 6 I Can Play Basketball P. 84	Different sports	Present continuous (all forms), -ing spelling rules, short answers, ordinal numbers	Brazilian soccer player, Marta Discussion about breaking the rules	On-line profile Produce an on-line profile	Fair play

REVIEW — Units 5 and 6 - p. 98 and 99

	WORD WORK	FOCUS ON LANGUAGE	LISTEN AND SPEAK	READ AND WRITE	TIPS FOR LIFE
UNIT 7 You Are What You Eat P. 100	Food: fruit, vegetables and dairy products, numbers 1 to 3,000	Regular and irregular plurals, demonstrative pronouns (this, that, these, those), simple present (all forms), short answers	Prepare a recipe and an interview about healthy food Play a fun game	Supermarket flyer Create a special flyer	Healthy habits
UNIT 8 Let's Go Camping! P. 114	Camping activities and items	Third person singular – spelling rules, third person simple present, short answers, adverbs of frequency	A camping trip to the mountains Describe the daily routine at a camping site	Packing list for camping Produce a packing list	Respect rules: good camping manners

REVIEW — Units 7 and 8 - p. 128 and 129

EXTRA PRACTICE P. 130
PROJECTS P. 138
FUN ACTIVITIES P. 142
GLOSSARY P. 146
GRAMMAR HELPER P. 151
WORKBOOK P. 161

WELCOME!

POLITE WORDS

Hello e Hi são formas de cumprimento, porém Hi é mais informal.

1 Match the columns.

a. Say Hello
b. Say Goodbye
c. Say Please
d. Say Sorry
e. Say Thank you
f. Say You're welcome

◯ when someone helps you or does you a favor.
◯ when you're wrong.
◯ when someone thanks you for doing something.
◯ when you are leaving.
◯ when you meet or greet someone.
◯ when you request something to be done.

THE ALPHABET

2 Say the alphabet.

A B C D E F G H I J K L M
N O P Q R S T U V W X Y Z

passion artist/Shutterstock

No inglês norte-americano, a letra "Z" é pronunciada /zi/ enquanto no inglês britânico e no inglês falado no Canadá é pronunciada /zed/.
Ao soletrar palavras contendo duas consoantes seguidas, como *apple*, falamos "A-*double*-P-L-E". Ao soletrar *Harry*, falamos "H-A-*double*-R-Y".

NUMBERS 1 TO 100

3 Write the missing numbers. Then listen and check.

| thirty-four | four | nine | eleven | thirty-one | fourteen | thirty-two |
| twenty | twelve | twenty-four | seventy | a hundred | thirty-three |

0 zero	1 one	2 two	3 three	4 _____	5 five
6 six	7 seven	8 eight	9 _____	10 ten	11 _____
12 _____	13 thirteen	14 _____	15 fifteen	16 sixteen	17 seventeen
18 eighteen	19 nineteen	20 _____	21 twenty-one	22 twenty-two	23 twenty-three
24 _____	25 twenty-five	26 twenty-six	27 twenty-seven	28 twenty-eight	29 twenty-nine
30 thirty	31 _____	32 _____	33 _____	34 _____	40 forty
50 fifty	60 sixty	70 _____	80 eighty	90 ninety	100 _____

4 Check the correct spelling of the numbers.

20	8	90	55
○ twelve	○ eighteen	○ nineteen	○ fifty-five
○ twenty	○ eight	○ ninety	○ fifteen
43	**60**	**17**	**70**
○ forty	○ sixty	○ seven	○ seventeen
○ forty-three	○ sixteen	○ seventeen	○ seventy
100	**3**	**80**	**30**
○ a hundred	○ thirteen	○ eighty	○ thirteen
○ a thousand	○ three	○ eighteen	○ thirty

Now, answer the question:

How old are you? I am _____ years old.

DAYS OF THE WEEK AND MONTHS

5 Complete the missing letters. Then listen and practice the days of the week.

a. 😐 WE____NESDA____

b. ☺ T____U____SDAY

c. 😴 ____ON____AY

d. 😎 SA____U____DAY

e. 🙄 TU____S____AY

f. 😍 FR____D____Y

g. 😊 S____N____AY

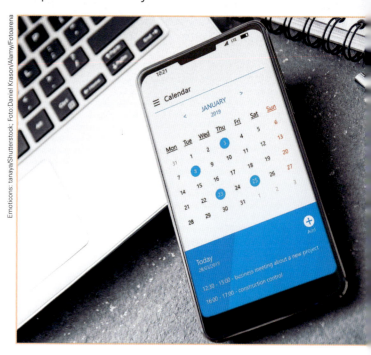

LANGUAGE TIPS

Em inglês, os dias da semana e o nome dos meses são sempre escritos em letras iniciais maiúsculas, ao contrário do português. Nos Estados Unidos e Canadá, a semana começa no domingo (*Sunday*) e não na segunda-feira, como na América do Sul, Reino Unido, Austrália, Irlanda e África do Sul. Para ler mais, acesse o *site*: <https://www.infoescola.com/ingles/dias-da-semana-em-ingles/>. Acesso em: 1º out. 2018.

6 Now, write the days of the week in order.

_____

7 Find the months of the year and color. Then practice saying them.

P	J	A	N	U	A	R	Y	B	C	I
O	E	D	E	M	A	J	U	J	A	S
C	F	E	T	A	U	U	U	U	N	E
T	G	C	Y	P	G	M	A	L	S	P
O	F	E	B	R	U	A	R	Y	T	T
B	E	M	O	I	S	Y	D	J	U	E
E	A	B	A	L	T	J	U	L	R	M
R	M	E	O	W	T	U	B	Q	Y	B
M	A	R	C	H	P	E	R	J	A	E
A	B	A	N	O	V	E	M	B	E	R

8 Answer: What's your favorite color? _____

SCHOOL OBJECTS

9 Match the school objects. Then listen and say.

a. pencil case
b. eraser
c. schoolbag
d. highlighter
e. mechanical pencil
f. scissors
g. ruler
h. notebook
i. glue stick
j. pen
k. pencil
l. pencil sharpener

10 In pairs, ask and answer: What's in your schoolbag?

11 In pairs, number the pictures according to the classroom commands. Then listen and repeat.

TIME FOR A GAME

Let's play **Sausage Game** and **Chinese Whisper**!

1. Read the text.
2. Close your book.
3. Come to the board.
4. Can you repeat it, please?
5. Be quiet, please!
6. Don't cheat!
7. How do you say "*régua*" in English?
8. Can you help me, please?
9. Open your books to page 10.
10. May I go to the restroom?
11. Work in groups.
12. Please, stand up/sit down.
13. Listen to the audio.
14. Write the answers in your notebook.

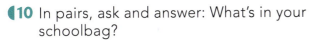

Unit 1 A GLOBAL WORLD

◀1 Look at the picture. Is it a big city?

◀2 Read and listen to the dialog. Then act out.

🔊8 **Kitty:** Hello! My name is Katherine, but please call me Kitty. What's your name?

Sayuri: Hi, Kitty. I'm Sayuri.

Kitty: Nice to meet you virtually, Sayuri.

Sayuri: Nice to meet you, too, Kitty. It's nice to have a new friend. By the way, where are you from, Kitty?

Kitty: I'm from New York. I'm American! And you, where are you from, Sayuri?

Sayuri: I'm from Tokyo. I'm Japanese. How old are you, Kitty?

Kitty: I'm eleven. How old are you, Sayuri?

Sayuri: I'm twelve.

Kitty: Now we are virtual friends.

Sayuri: Yes! We are e-pals now!

Kitty: Where are you now?

Sayuri: I'm at school. And you?

Kitty: I'm at home. Talk to you soon.

Sayuri: Yes. Bye-bye!

◀3 Read the dialog again and answer.

a. Who is Sayuri?
   ○ Sayuri is Kitty's e-pal.
   ○ Sayuri is Kitty's classmate.

b. Where is she from?
   ○ She is from the USA.
   ○ She is from Japan.

ELEVEN 11

THINKING AHEAD

1 Listen and number the pictures.

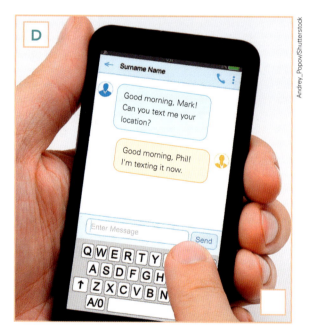

2 In pairs, match the descriptions to the pictures from activity 1.

a. ◯ a text message

b. ◯ a face-to-face conversation

c. ◯ a cell phone call

d. ◯ a call with audio and video chat on the internet

A WORD WORK

1 🔊 10 Where are they from? Listen, complete and check.

American	Australian	Brazilian	Canadian
Chinese	English	French	German
Japanese	Mexican	Nigerian	South Korean

TO LEARN MORE

Remember, in English, nationalities are always written with a capital letter.

Brazil
Brazilian

South Korea
_____

Australia
_____

Canada
_____

China
_____

England
_____

Nigeria
_____

Germany
_____

Japan
_____

Mexico
_____

France
_____

the USA
_____

ENGLISH PLUS

To learn more about other countries, nationalities and flags, go to: <https://www.gov.uk/government/publications/nationalities/list-of-nationalities>. Accessed on: Dec. 14, 2018.

12 Find five nationalities in the word search. Then complete the sentences using them.

a. Brigitte is from France. She is _____.

b. Radhi is from Nigeria. He is _____.

c. Ana Maria is from Brazil. She is _____.

d. Steve is from England. He is _____.

e. Luna is from Mexico. She is _____.

13 Look at the flags and complete the sentences. Where is each flag from?

1
2
3
4
5

6
7
8
9
10

TIME FOR A GAME

Let's play **Call the Number** and **The Alphabet Game**!

FOCUS ON LANGUAGE

1 In pairs, compare the sentences and complete.

Amu is from Nigeria. _____ is Nigerian.

Bob and **Jane** are fifty. _____ are my parents.

2 Look at the picture. Then read the chart.

Subject Pronouns							
Singular				Plural			
I	You	He	She	It	We	You	They

Go to page 151.

Verb to be – Present tense		
Affirmative		
Subject Pronouns	Verb to be (long forms)	Contracted forms (short forms)
I	am	'm	from Brazil.
You	are	're	twelve years old.
He/She/It	is	's	in the garden.
We/You/They	are	're	at home.

3 Look at the picture. Then complete the sentences with **am**, **is** or **are**.

a. I _____ Lang Cheng. This _____ my family.

b. We _____ from Shanghai in China. We _____ Chinese.

c. Liu Yang _____ my son. He _____ six years old.

d. My wife _____ an English teacher.

e. Now we _____ in Chinatown.

4 Read and match the columns.

a. Kangaroos and koalas are from Australia.   ◯ He's a teenager.

b. Joe is thirteen years old.   ◯ It's new.

c. Marta is a great soccer player.   ◯ We're good students.

d. Kitty and I are virtual friends.   ◯ She's Brazilian.

e. My digital camera is from Japan.   ◯ They're marsupials.

5 Takao meets a new classmate and asks her some questions. Check the correct answers.

a. What is your name?
   ◯ I'm Sandy.
   ◯ I'm Chinese.

b. Where are you from?
   ◯ My name is Chan.
   ◯ I'm from Canada.

c. Nice to meet you.
   ◯ Hello, I'm Takao.
   ◯ Nice to meet you, too.

d. How old are you?
   ◯ I'm twelve years old.
   ◯ I come from China.

6 Read the dialog and complete it.

Takao: Hello, my name is Takao. What is your name?

New student: My name is _____.

Takao: I'm from Japan. I'm Japanese. Where are you from?

New student: I'm from _____. I'm _____.

Takao: Now we are friends. Nice to meet you.

New student: _____, too, Takao.

Takao: Talk to you soon.

New student: _____.

7 Read and complete the sentences with **am**, **is** or **are**.

a. You _____ a teacher.
○ is   ○ are   ○ am

b. It _____ a big dog.
○ am   ○ is   ○ are

c. Tommy and Steve _____ best friends.
○ are   ○ is   ○ am

d. My friend _____ twelve years old.
○ am   ○ are   ○ is

e. I _____ from Toronto, Canada.
○ is   ○ am   ○ are

8 Read the internet profiles and write full sentences.

First name: Tyler
Last name: Smith
Age: 12
Country: England
Nationality: English

My name is Tyler Smith.
I'm twelve (years old).
I'm from England.
I'm English.

First name: Hope
Last name: Nkosi
Age: 15
Country: South Africa
Nationality: South African

_____
_____
_____
_____

First name: Oliver
Last name: Williams
Age: 13
Country: Australia
Nationality: Australian

_____
_____
_____
_____

First name: Zhao
Last name: Wang
Age: 11
Country: China
Nationality: Chinese

_____
_____
_____
_____

LISTEN AND SPEAK

1 Look and label the pictures. Then listen and repeat.
🔊 11

| Good afternoon | Good evening | Good morning | Good night |

a.

b.

_____

c.

d.

_____

2 Listen to the dialogs and complete with the correct greetings.
🔊 12

a.
Hello, Carol!
_____, Kitty!

b.
Bye, Mom!
_____, Leo!

c.
_____, Jim!
Good morning, Leo!

d.
Good afternoon, Lauryn!
_____, Liz!

3 Three students are at the International Green School. They are answering some questions about themselves. Listen and check the answers.

a. In Dialog 1, the student's name is Arjun and he is _____.
   ◯ Italian   ◯ Indian   ◯ Iranian

b. In Dialog 2, the student's name is _____. She is _____.
   ◯ Amahle/South African   ◯ Marie/French   ◯ Amahle/Cuban

c. In Dialog 3, the student's name is _____. He is _____.
   ◯ Carlos/Nigerian   ◯ Liam/New Zealander   ◯ Carlos/New Zealander

4 In pairs, talk to a classmate.

a. What is your first name? My first name is…
b. What is your last name? My last name is…
c. Where are you from? I'm from…
d. How old are you? I'm…

PRONUNCIATION CORNER

1 Listen and say the tongue twister.

They are the three funny frogs.
They are from France.
They are French.
They are free, they are free!
The three funny frogs are free!

2 Listen and circle the word you hear.

thin	fin
death	deaf
thought	fought
myth	Miffy

CROSS CULTURAL

O *site* <https://mashable.com/2015/03/15/greetings-around-the-world/#f9eHPYcEbOq0> (acesso em: 17 dez. 2018) oferece um infográfico representando 15 formas diferentes de se cumprimentar pessoas ao redor do mundo.

Frido Nesti/Arquivo da editora

READ AND WRITE

1. Look at the pictures and the text.

   a. What are they doing?
   - ○ They are chatting.
   - ○ They are playing video game.

   b. What is the text about?
   - ○ It's about two virtual friends.
   - ○ It's about two school colleagues.

2. Now read the text.

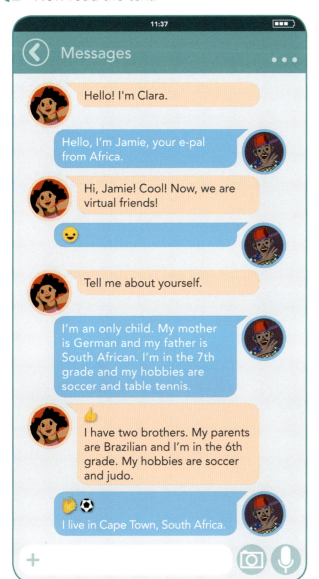

3. Read the text again and check the correct sentences.

   a. ○ Jamie is from Cape Town, in South Africa.

   b. ○ Clara is in the 7th grade at school.

   c. ○ Clara and Jamie are e-pals.

   d. ○ Jamie speaks English and Afrikaans.

TWENTY-ONE 21

14 Imagine you are chatting with Clara or Jamie, your new e-pal. Introduce yourself. Write a message asking questions and sharing some information about you. Follow the steps.

  a. Choose the person you want to send the message to.
  b. Remember to use digital language: emojis, emoticons, abbreviations, acronyms etc.
  c. Plan what you want to write to this e-pal to be posted in the chat group.
  d. Write a draft of it in your notebook.
  e. Show it to your teacher and make the necessary corrections.
  f. Then write the final version of the message in your book.

15 Now share your message with your classmates and teacher.

TIPS FOR LIFE

Respect diversity

1 Read the text and the poster.

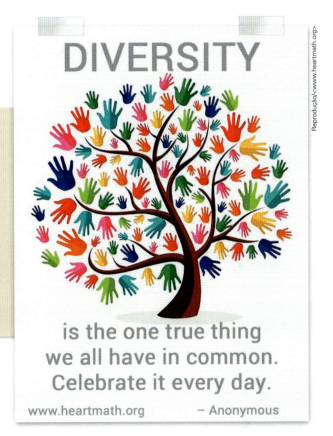

It doesn't matter what you look like, what your race is, where you are from, what religion you practice, what you eat, what your preferences are, features of your culture etc.

It's not right to judge people. Everyone is unique and that's great!

Based on: <https://www.debate.org/opinions/it-doesnt-matter-what-you-look-like-where-you-come-from-what-religion-you-follow-or-the-color-of-your-skin-were-all-human-beings>. Accessed on: Dec. 14, 2018.

2 Close your eyes! Imagine a world where people are alike. Choose words from the box to write and draw about it.

| sad | funny | boring | interesting | not |
| interesting | happy | nice | ridiculous | unhappy |

CHECK YOUR PROGRESS	😃	😐	☹️
Greetings / nationalities			
Subject pronouns			
Verb to be			
Listening			
Speaking			
Reading			
Writing			

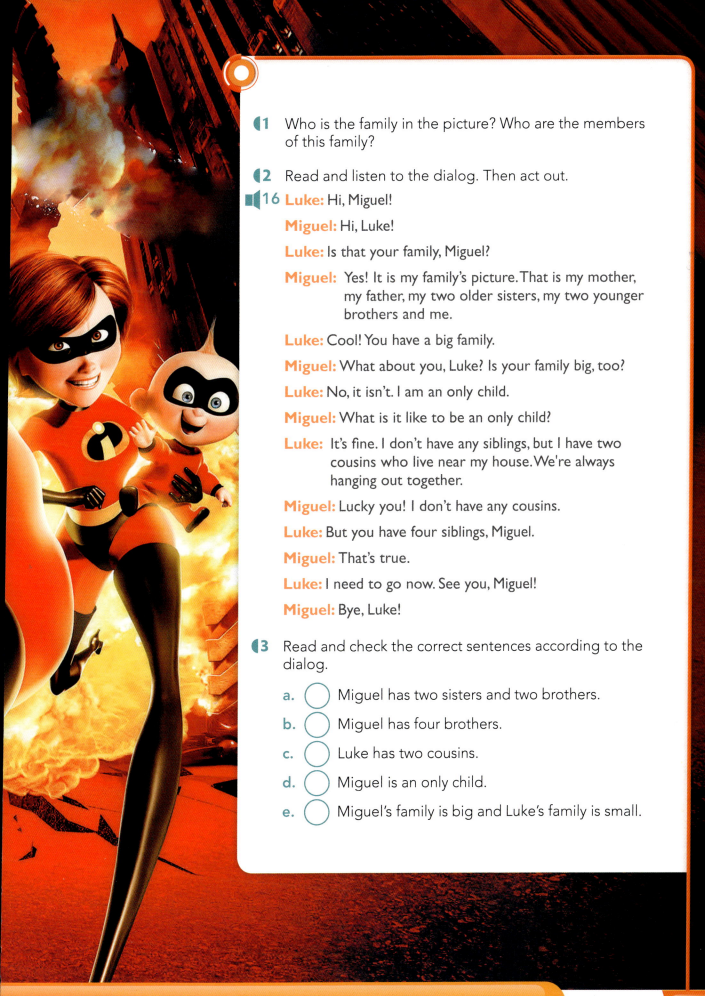

1 Who is the family in the picture? Who are the members of this family?

2 Read and listen to the dialog. Then act out.

16 **Luke:** Hi, Miguel!

Miguel: Hi, Luke!

Luke: Is that your family, Miguel?

Miguel: Yes! It is my family's picture. That is my mother, my father, my two older sisters, my two younger brothers and me.

Luke: Cool! You have a big family.

Miguel: What about you, Luke? Is your family big, too?

Luke: No, it isn't. I am an only child.

Miguel: What is it like to be an only child?

Luke: It's fine. I don't have any siblings, but I have two cousins who live near my house. We're always hanging out together.

Miguel: Lucky you! I don't have any cousins.

Luke: But you have four siblings, Miguel.

Miguel: That's true.

Luke: I need to go now. See you, Miguel!

Miguel: Bye, Luke!

3 Read and check the correct sentences according to the dialog.

a. ◯ Miguel has two sisters and two brothers.
b. ◯ Miguel has four brothers.
c. ◯ Luke has two cousins.
d. ◯ Miguel is an only child.
e. ◯ Miguel's family is big and Luke's family is small.

TWENTY-FIVE **25**

THINKING AHEAD

1 Number the definitions according to the pictures. Follow the example.

1

nuclear family

2

single parent family

3

extended family

4

childless family

5

step family

6

grandparent family

(3) A family that includes grandparents, uncles or aunts.

( ) A family in which there is a step-parent.

( ) A grandfather (or grandmother) and grandchildren.

( ) Only a couple.

( ) A single parent (father or mother) and children.

( ) A couple and children.

2 According to the dialog on the previous page, what is Miguel's kind of family? Discuss with your classmates.

ENGLISH PLUS

Para complementar a aula e inspirar a conversa com seus pais a respeito da história deles e de seus avós, bisavós, etc., assista ao vídeo *Eu*, do grupo Palavra Cantada. Duração: 4 min 3 s. Disponível em: <www.youtube.com/watch?v=2cqcWHs7a_E>. Acesso em: 21 dez. 2018.

A WORD WORK

1 Look at the picture: who are they?

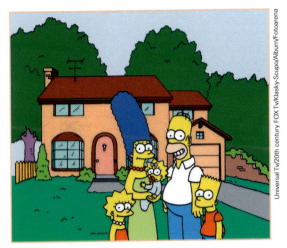

CROSS CULTURAL

The Simpsons é uma série estadunidense, criada por Matt Groening em 1989, que faz uma sátira do estilo de vida da classe média dos Estados Unidos ao contar a história de Homer Jay Simpson, Marjorie (Marge) Bouvier Simpson, Bartholomew (Bart) Simpson, Elisabeth (Lisa) Marie Simpson e Margareth (Maggie) Simpson.

2 Now, look at their family tree and complete the gaps.

| mother | father | brother | sister | grandmother |
| grandfather | uncle | aunt | cousin |

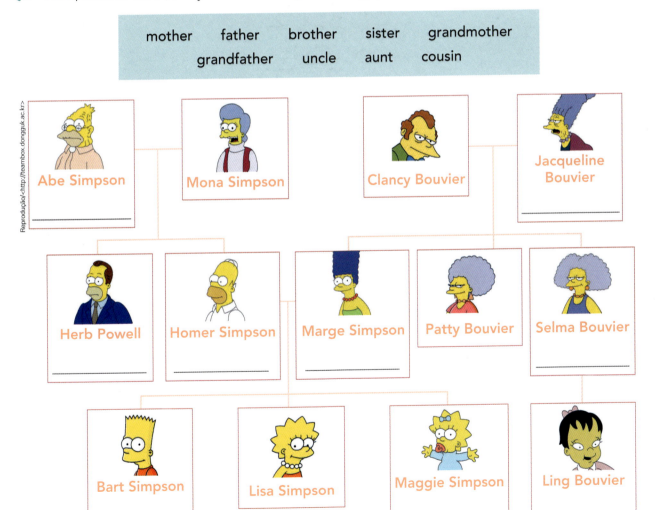

3 In pairs, listen, complete and say. Who are they?

🔊 17 a. Mona is Bart's grandmother.

b. _____ is Homer's father.

c. _____ is Clancy's wife.

d. _____ is Lisa's grandfather.

e. _____ is Marge's husband.

f. _____ is Homer's brother and Bart's uncle.

g. _____ is Abe's son.

h. _____ is Jacqueline's daughter.

i. _____ is Lisa's uncle.

j. _____ is Ling's mother.

k. _____ is Maggie's cousin.

l. _____ is Mona's granddaughter.

m. _____ is Patty's niece.

n. _____ is Selma's nephew.

o. _____ is Clancy's grandson.

ENGLISH PLUS

To draw your own family tree, you can access the website FamilySearch at <https://www.familysearch.org/search/family-trees>. Accessed on: Dec. 19, 2018.

4 Now, answer the questions about yourself. What is/are your…

a. father's name? _____

b. mother's name? _____

c. siblings' names? _____

d. cousins' names? _____

TIME FOR A GAME

Let's play **Hangman** and **Spelling Bee**!

FOCUS ON LANGUAGE

1 Read the comic strip and underline an affirmative and an interrogative sentence with verb **to be**.

2 Read the chart and write the sentences in the interrogative form.

> Affirmative form: **He** + **is** + in the living room.
>
> Interrogative form: **Is** + **he** + in the living room?

a. Emily and Susan are at school now.

_____

b. The English book is in Emma's bedroom.

_____

c. The name of the boy is Charlie Brown.

_____

d. Lucy is in the kitchen.

_____

3 Read the chart below.

Verb to be – Negative		
Long forms	**Contracted forms (short forms)**	
I **am not**	I'm not	in the kitchen.
You **are not**	You aren't	
He/She/It **is not**	He/She/It isn't	
We/You/They **are not**	We/You/They aren't	

Go to page 152.

4 Look at Edward Hopper's painting. Then rewrite the sentences using the correct information. Follow the example.

Edward Hopper (1882-1967), pintor, artista gráfico e ilustrador estadunidense, é famoso por suas obras que representam vividamente a solidão em tempos contemporâneos. Ele recriou cenários urbanos e rurais que refletem a visão dele da vida moderna nos Estados Unidos.

Chop Suey. Edward Hopper, 1929.

The woman's dress is red.
The woman's dress isn't red. It's green.

a. The tables are blue.

_____

b. The women's hats are yellow.

_____

c. It is a dancing club.

_____

d. The man's suit is gray.

_____

5 Read and complete the answers using the short forms of the verb *to be*. Follow the example.

a. Are the curtains in the windows black?
No, they aren't.

b. Is Robert eating in the kitchen?

No, _____.

c. Is the lamp's light green?

Yes, _____.

d. Are we late for school?

Yes, _____.

Verb to be – Short answers

	Affirmative	Negative
I	Yes, I am.	No, I'm not.
You	Yes, you are.	No, you aren't.
He, She, It	Yes, (he) is.	No, (he) isn't.
We, You, They	Yes, (we) are.	No, (we) aren't.

GRAMMAR HELPER

Go to page 152.

16 Look at the pictures and read the chart.

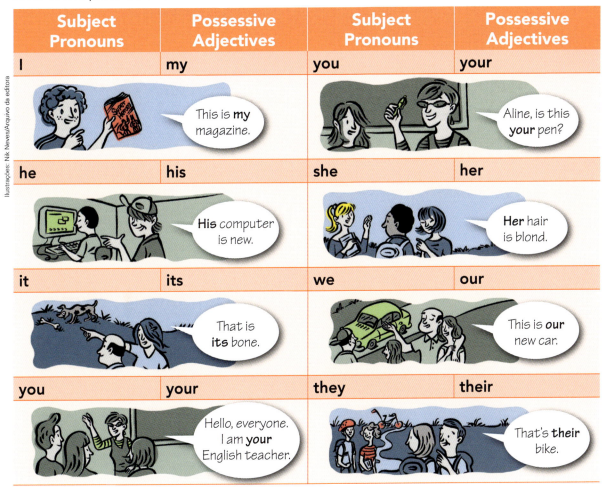

17 Complete Amy's e-mail with Subject Pronouns or Possessive Adjectives.

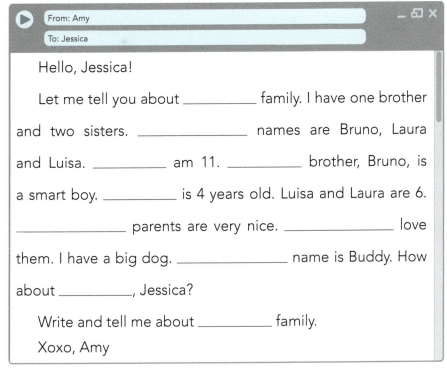

Hello, Jessica!

Let me tell you about _____ family. I have one brother and two sisters. _____ names are Bruno, Laura and Luisa. _____ am 11. _____ brother, Bruno, is a smart boy. _____ is 4 years old. Luisa and Laura are 6. _____ parents are very nice. _____ love them. I have a big dog. _____ name is Buddy. How about _____, Jessica?

Write and tell me about _____ family.
Xoxo, Amy

GRAMMAR HELPER

Go to page 153.

8   Read Jessica's e-mail and circle: whose cat is this?

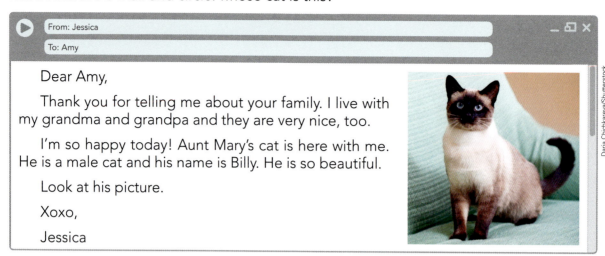

From: Jessica
To: Amy

Dear Amy,

Thank you for telling me about your family. I live with my grandma and grandpa and they are very nice, too.

I'm so happy today! Aunt Mary's cat is here with me. He is a male cat and his name is Billy. He is so beautiful.

Look at his picture.

Xoxo,

Jessica

9   Read the chart and answer the questions.

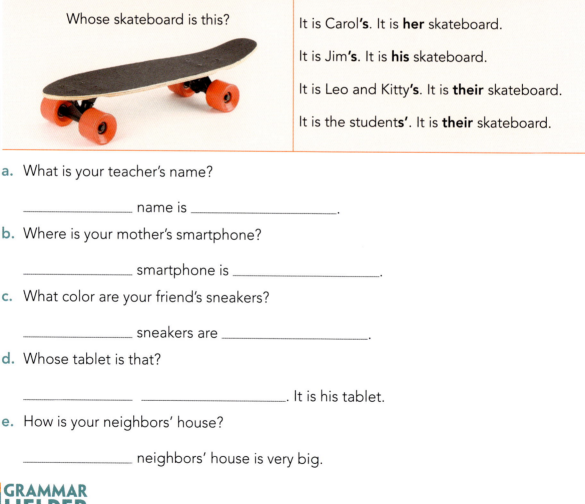

Genitive Case ('s)

Whose skateboard is this?

It is Carol**'s**. It is **her** skateboard.

It is Jim**'s**. It is **his** skateboard.

It is Leo and Kitty**'s**. It is **their** skateboard.

It is the students**'**. It is **their** skateboard.

a. What is your teacher's name?

   _____ name is _____.

b. Where is your mother's smartphone?

   _____ smartphone is _____.

c. What color are your friend's sneakers?

   _____ sneakers are _____.

d. Whose tablet is that?

   _____ _____. It is his tablet.

e. How is your neighbors' house?

   _____ neighbors' house is very big.

GRAMMAR HELPER

Go to page 153.

LISTEN AND SPEAK

1. Listen to Namazzi and circle the words related to her family members mentioned.

   | cousin | Africa | brothers | Uganda | father |
   | mother | water | sister | village | parents |

2. Now, listen to Namazzi again and answer **T** (true) or **F** (false).
   a. ◯ Namazzi is from the Republic of Congo, in Africa.
   b. ◯ She is in the 7th grade.
   c. ◯ She is 13 years old.
   d. ◯ In her language, her name means "sun".
   e. ◯ When she grows up, she wants to be a doctor.

3. Listen to Namazzi one more time and fill in the gaps.
   a. I live with my _____, my _____, and my two younger _____.
   b. I live in a small village in _____, Africa.
   c. My great wish is to build a permanent _____ for my _____ and my brothers.
   d. When I grow up, I want to be a nurse and help other _____.

Some children from Africa and many other countries are sponsored by humanitarian organizations such as Plan International. These organizations work to improve their livelihoods and offer them health, education and protection. To know more about Plan International, access: <www.plan.ie/>. To know Matheo and other sponsored children, access: <www.youtube.com/watch?v=rLldSLXEa9M>. Accessed on: Dec. 21, 2018.

4 Listen to Edward talk about his family. Then complete his family tree using the names from the box.

> Ellen   Virginia   Edward   George   Phillip
> Loretta   Beth   Ferdinand   Nicholas

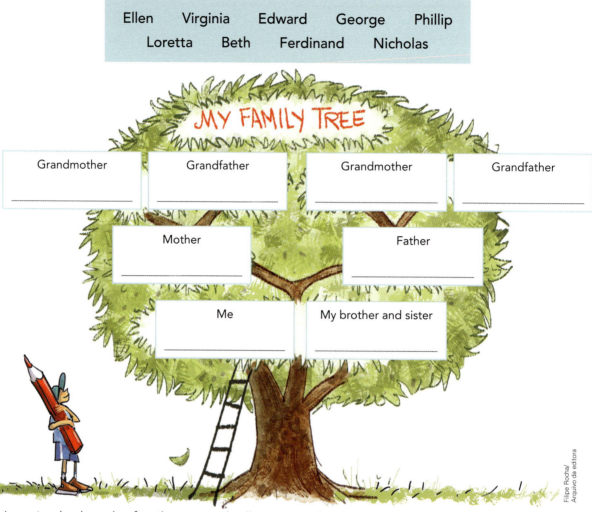

5 In pairs, look at the family tree and talk to your classmates.

a. Who are Edward's family members?

b. How about you? Who are your family members?

PRONUNCIATION CORNER

1 Listen and say the tongue twister.

Happy Harry has long hair,
he is happy and honest.
He is from Hillsdorf.
His father, Henry,
is from Helsinki.
Harry and Henry live in a
small house.
Hello, Harry!
Hello, Henry!

2 Repeat the words.

happy hour
have honor
be honest
hundred
husband
his/her

READ AND WRITE

1 Read the title, look at the picture and answer: who is this boy?

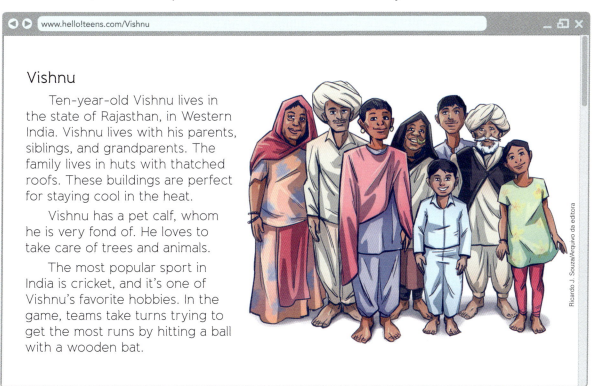

Vishnu

Ten-year-old Vishnu lives in the state of Rajasthan, in Western India. Vishnu lives with his parents, siblings, and grandparents. The family lives in huts with thatched roofs. These buildings are perfect for staying cool in the heat.

Vishnu has a pet calf, whom he is very fond of. He loves to take care of trees and animals.

The most popular sport in India is cricket, and it's one of Vishnu's favorite hobbies. In the game, teams take turns trying to get the most runs by hitting a ball with a wooden bat.

Based on:: SAUNDERS, Catherine; PRIDDY, Sam; LENNON, Katy. *Children Just Like Me*. DK Publishing, New York, 2016. Page 61.

2 Complete the sentences using information from the text.

a. Vishnu lives in Rajasthan, _____.

b. Vishnu lives with his _____.

c. Vishnu has a brother and _____.

d. Vishnu has a pet _____.

e. One of Vishnu's favorite hobbies/sports is _____.

f. Vishnu is _____ years old.

3 Now, in pairs, talk about the text.

a. What are your impressions about the text?

b. What family members does Vishnu live with? How about you?

c. In your opinion, what important information is missing from the text?

4 You will make a class presentation about a family member who is special to you. Think about some information you would like to share and write about him/her.

   a. Choose a special family member and write his/her definition in English (mother, father, brother etc.).

   b. Plan the information you want to share about him/her: age, job, personality, place where he/she lives, hobbies, the reason why he/she is special to you etc.

   c. Write a draft of the text in your notebook.

   d. Exchange it with a classmate and talk about some new ideas to add in your text.

   e. Show it to your teacher and make the necessary corrections.

   f. Then write the final version of the text in your book.

5 Now, select some pictures of your family member and make a presentation to your classmates.

TIPS FOR LIFE

Love and respect your family!

1. Look at the poster and read the sentences. Choose the top five in your opinion and create your own family rules poster.

Family Rules

say please and thank you
SHARE DON'T WHINE
kisses before bedtime
love one another
ALWAYS TELL THE TRUTH
say your prayers
DO YOUR CHORES
LAUGH use kind words
try new things
always say i love you
KEEP YOUR PROMISES
treat others how you want to be treated

Kapoors

MY FAMILY RULES

1. _____
2. _____
3. _____
4. _____
5. _____

CHECK YOUR PROGRESS	😃	😐	☹️
Family vocabulary			
Verb *to be* (interrogative and negative forms)			
Possessive Adjectives / Genitive Case ('s)			
Listening			
Speaking			
Reading			
Writing			

REVIEW

UNITS 1 AND 2

1 Look at the pictures and write the corresponding greetings.

a. b. c. d.

2 Complete the dialogs using the words from the box.

a. | hello | meet | name | nice |

Sandra: Hi, my _____ is Sandra.

Joshua: _____, Sandra! My name is Joshua.

_____ to meet you!

Sandra: Nice to _____ you, too.

b. | I'm | twelve | where | how |

Teacher: _____ are you from, Haruto?

Haruto: _____ from Tokyo, Japan.

Teacher: _____ old are you? Twelve?

Haruto: No, I'm not _____. I'm thirteen.

3 Complete the sentences with **am**, **is** or **are**.

a. Carmen _____ from Mexico. She _____ Mexican.

b. Cindy _____ thirteen years old and I _____ eleven.

c. Julia and I _____ e-pals. We _____ virtual friends.

d. Pierre and Patrick _____ brothers. They _____ from France.

e. Fernando _____ not from Chile. He _____ from Argentina.

f. I _____ not a student. I _____ a teacher.

4 Complete the gaps using **he's** or **she's** and nationalities.

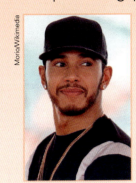

a. Where is Lewis Hamilton from? _____ from England. He's _____.

b. Marina Ruy Barbosa is an actress. _____ from Brazil. She's _____.

c. Hiroyuki Sanada is from Tokyo. _____ a famous _____ actor.

d. Ariana Grande is a singer and an actress. _____ from the United States. _____.

5 Complete the sentences with the words from the box.

| grandmother | uncle | grandfather | father | sister |
| mother | cousin | aunt | brother | |

a. My father's sister is my _____.

b. My father's mother is my _____.

c. My father's daughter is my _____.

d. My father's father is my _____.

e. My uncle's son is my _____.

f. My father's brother is my _____.

g. My father's son is my _____.

h. I'm his son. He is my _____.

i. I'm her daughter. She is my _____.

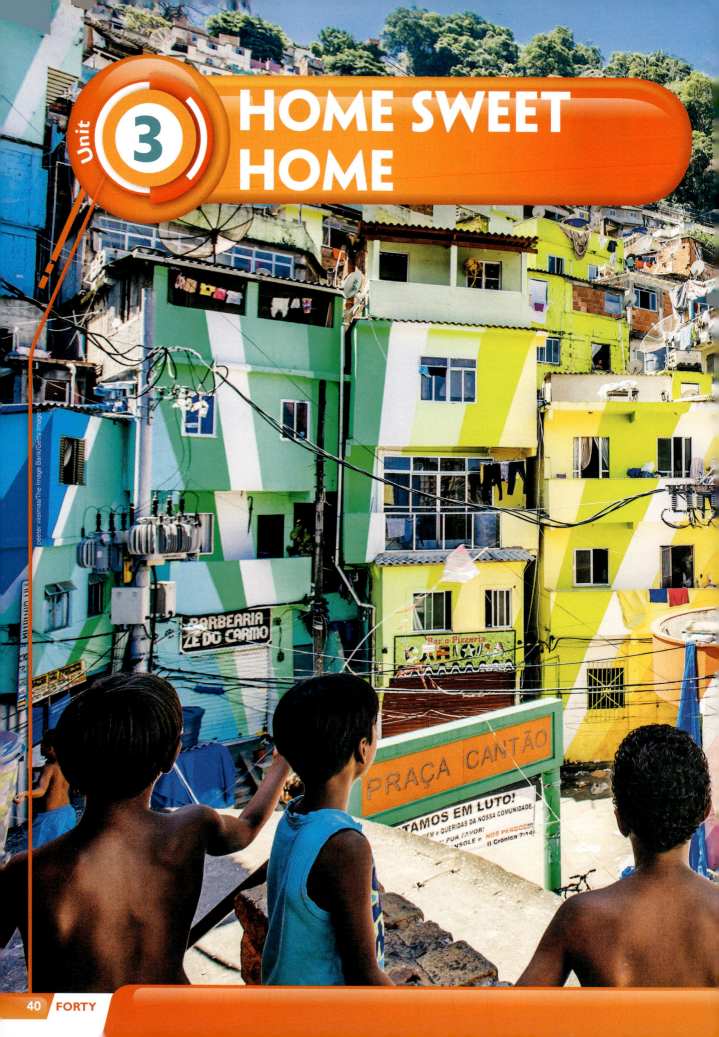

Unit 3 — HOME SWEET HOME

1. Look at the picture and talk to your classmates.

   a. What kinds of houses do you know?

   b. What does "Home Sweet Home" mean to you?

2. Read and listen to the dialog. Then act out.

   Woman: Hi, I'm interested in moving to a new house. Can you tell me about this one, please?

   Real estate agent: Hi, sure. It's a big house. There is a playroom, a living room, a dining room, an eating area, and a kitchen next to it. There are three bedrooms, and one of them is a master bedroom.

   Woman: How many bathrooms are there?

   Real estate agent: There are two bathrooms.

   Woman: Is this house furnished?

   Real estate agent: Yes, it is. There is furniture in the living room, a big and comfortable sofa, a TV stand and a coffee table. In the kitchen, there is a new fridge and a stove.

   Woman: Are there any beds in the bedroom?

   Real estate agent: In the master bedroom there is a large bed, but in the other ones there are only single beds.

   Woman: How many floors are there in this house? I'm looking for a one-story house.

   Real estate agent: There is just one floor. It's a beautiful one-story house with a big yard too.

   Woman: Great! Can I see the floor plan?

   Real estate agent: Yes, you can!

   Woman: Thank you!

3. Read the dialog again and answer **T** (True) or **F** (False).

   a. ◯ This house is quite small.

   b. ◯ There isn't a floor plan for this house.

   c. ◯ In this house, there are three bedrooms.

   d. ◯ There is a fridge and a stove in the kitchen.

THINKING AHEAD

1 Look at the one-story house below and its floor plan. Then do the activities.

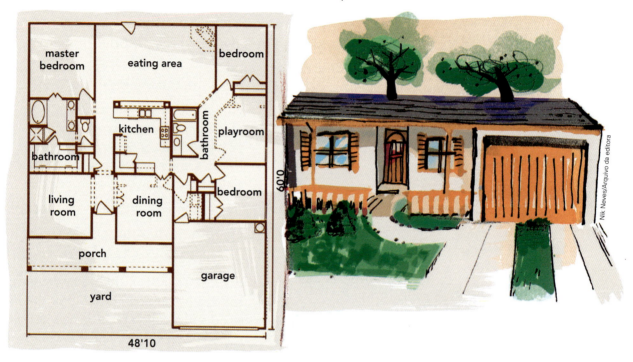

a. Draw the floor plan of your house.

b. Describe the floor plan of your house to a classmate.

 WORD WORK

1 Listen and repeat.

##

O nome dado à mobília e à decoração (*furnishings*) das casas pode variar de acordo com o país. Por exemplo, enquanto nos Estados Unidos o "fogão" é chamado de *stove*, na Inglaterra recebe o nome de *cooker*.

2 Circle the furnishings in activity 1 you find in your house. Then tell a classmate.

3 Complete the crossword.

TIME FOR A GAME

Let's play **Mime: "Where are you?"**, **Chinese Whisper**!

FOCUS ON LANGUAGE

1 In pairs, read the speech bubble below and do the activities.

There are three bedrooms in this house. There is a master bedroom, too.

a. Circle the sentence in singular.

b. Underline the sentence in plural.

2 Read the chart. Then complete the sentences with the words **affirmative**, **interrogative** or **negative**.

	There to be – Present		
	Affirmative	**Interrogative**	**Negative**
Singular	**There is** a fridge in the kitchen.	**Is there** a fridge in the kitchen?	**There isn't (is not)** a fridge in the kitchen.
Plural	**There are** two armchairs in the living room.	**Are there** two armchairs in the living room?	**There aren't (are not)** two armchairs in the living room.

a. We use **there is** and **there are** in _____ sentences.

b. We use **there isn't (is not)** and **there aren't (are not)** in _____ sentences.

c. We use **Is there** and **Are there** in _____ sentences.

Go to page 154.

3. Now, write three sentences about your classroom using **there is** and **there are**. Then ask a classmate to rewrite your sentences into the interrogative and negative forms.

_____
_____
_____

4. Look at the image and read the chart. Then answer the questions using **short answers**.

	There to be – Short answers	
	Affirmative	**Negative**
Singular	Yes, there is.	No, there isn't (is not).
Plural	Yes, there are.	No, there aren't (are not).

a. Is there a tablet in the kitchen?
_____

b. Are there plates on the table?
_____

c. Is there a telephone in the kitchen?
_____

d. Are there cabinets in the kitchen?
_____

CROSS CULTURAL

Nascido em Moscou, Rússia, em 1866, Wassily Kandinsky trabalhou na área jurídica até os 30 anos, quando decidiu se voltar para o mundo das artes. Após frequentar a Academia Real, na Alemanha, Kandinsky deu início a uma frutífera carreira, que fez dele um dos principais nomes do Expressionismo.

Elaborado com base em: <www.mac.usp.br/mac/templates/projetos/percursos/percursos_fig_abst_biog_kandinsky.asp>. Acesso em: 20 dez. 2018.

5 Look at the painting by Wassily Kandinsky. Then complete the sentences with the words from the box.

| Bedroom in Aintmillerstrasse   Kandinsky   Russian   yellow |

Bedroom in Aintmillerstrasse, 1909. Municipal Gallery in Lenbach House, Munich.

About the painting…

The name of the painting is
_____
_____.

The predominant color of the painting is
_____.

The painter's name is _____.

He is a _____ painter.

6 Complete the sentences about the painting with **there is**, **there are**, **there isn't** or **there aren't**.

a. _____ plates on the table.

b. _____ a single bed and a pillow.

c. _____ chairs. _____ a table.

d. _____ curtains. They're orange.

e. _____ a night table with a lamp on it.

f. _____ a door. _____ an open window.

7 Read the text and answer the questions.

> Hi, my name is Michael. I live in an apartment with my parents and my brother, David. I share a bedroom with him because there are only two bedrooms in my house. In our bedroom, there are three beds, because our cousin Tom always sleeps there!

a. How many bedrooms are there in Michael's house?

There are _____ bedrooms in Michael's house.

b. How many beds are there in his bedroom?

There are _____ beds in his bedroom.

8 Read the sentences and circle the correct option.

> **Woman:** How many bathrooms are there in this house?
>
> **Real estate agent:** There are two bathrooms.
>
> We use **how many** when we want to know about the quantity/quality of something.

9 Look at the picture and answer the following questions.

a. How many armchairs are there in the living room?

_____

b. How many cushions are there on the armchairs?

_____

c. How many yellow cushions are there in the picture?

_____

10 Write two questions using **how many**. Ask a classmate to answer them.

_____

_____

LISTEN AND SPEAK

1 Listen to the conversation and circle the numbers.
🔊 26

2 Listen to the real estate agent and circle the correct answers.
🔊 27

a. The real estate agent is selling **an old/a new house**.

b. The house is on **Malibu Road/Victoria Road**.

c. The house has **three/four** bedrooms.

d. It includes a **home theater/air conditioning**.

e. The kitchen has a **fridge/microwave oven**.

3 Think about your dream house and draw it. Then talk to a classmate about it.

1 Listen and act out the jazz chant.

🔊 28
- **A:** Where are you, Jim?
- **B:** I'm in the kitchen.
- **A:** In the kitchen?
- **B:** Yes, talking on the phone.
- **A:** Where are you, Mr. Blackmoon?
- **C:** I'm in the bedroom.
- **A:** Where are you, John?
- **D:** I'm in Rome.

2 Listen and repeat.

🔊 29

| bathroom | woman | dining room |
| in | Jim | garden |

READ AND WRITE

1 Read the text. It's an example of an

a. ( ) article about houses on sale.   b. ( ) online ad about a cottage for rent.

Where

Minden Hills, Ontario, Canada

Cottage for rent!

Furnished, three bedrooms (1 bdrm. double bed/ 2 bdrm. 2 single beds) and 2 bath. with tub and shower, modern kitchen with all appliances, including microwave oven. Comfortable living room, great lake view. Wood and gas fireplace and a gas barbecue grill. Heat, color cable television, wireless internet access. Prkg.

Call (416) 563-4775. C$ 530 (min. 7 nights).

CROSS CULTURAL

A moeda oficial do Canadá é o **dólar canadense** ou **dólar canadiano**. Em circulação desde 1858, ela costuma ser representada pelo símbolo C$ ou Can$.

Baseado em: <www.terravista.pt/717/dolar-canadiano.html>. Acesso em: 4 jan. 2019.

2 Check all the elements you can find in this text.

a. ( ) Price.   d. ( ) Owners' name.
b. ( ) Location.   e. ( ) Contact information.
c. ( ) Client review.   f. ( ) Description of the cottage.

3 Match the abbreviations.

bdrm.   parking
min.   bathroom
prkg.   bedroom
bath.   minimal

4 Answer the questions.

a. Where is the cottage located?
___

b. What is the title of the ad?
___

c. Which rooms of the house are mentioned?
___

d. How many beds are there in the bedrooms?
___

5 Imagine you want to sell or rent your dream house. Write an online ad for it following these steps:

a. Write your dream house based on your answers in activity 2.

b. Use a dictionary to complement the description of your house.

c. Write a draft.

d. Show it to your teacher and make the necessary corrections.

e. Then write the final version on a sheet of paper – don't forget the image.

TIPS FOR LIFE

Cooperation: helping with the house chores

1 Do you usually help your family with the household chores?

○ Yes   ○ No

2 Check the chores you usually do at home.

a.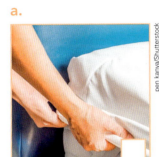
Make the bed

b.
Sweep the floor

c.
Do the dishes

d.
Take out the garbage

e.
Set the table

f.
Tidy up the table after meals

g.
Do the vacuuming

h.
Do the laundry

3 Share with your classmates the chores you do at home.

CHECK YOUR PROGRESS	😀	😐	☹️
Rooms of the house and furnishings			
There to be			
Listening			
Speaking			
Reading			
Writing			

Unit 4: GETTING AROUND TOWN

1. Look at the picture and talk to your classmates.

   a. In your opinion, is this city big or small? Why?

   b. What is there to visit?

2. Read and listen to the dialog. Then act out.

Allan: Leo, we are lost. We should ask for directions to get to Central Stadium.

Leo: There is a police officer next to the restaurant. Let's talk to him.

Leo: Excuse me, sir. Can you help us, please? Where is the Central Stadium?

Cop: Oh! It's not far from here, kids. It's at 1450 Main Street.

Allan: How do we get there?

Cop: It's easy, son. Go straight ahead two blocks on Kipling Avenue, turn right on Main Street, walk two blocks, and Central Stadium is on your left, right next to the Plaza Hotel. You can't miss it!

Kids: Great! Thank you, sir.

Cop: You're welcome, kids.

Kitty: What time is it now, Leo?

Leo: It's five o'clock, Kitty.

Allan: Are we late for the rock concert, Leo?

Leo: Yes, we are a little late. Let's go!

Kitty: Hey, guys! Wait for me!

3. Read the sentences and check the correct ones.

   a. ◯ Leo, Allan and Kitty are going to Central Stadium.

   b. ◯ They ask for directions to get to the stadium.

   c. ◯ They talk to a doctor on the street.

   d. ◯ The stadium is next to the Plaza Hotel.

THINKING AHEAD

1 Look at the city map from where Leo, Kitty and Allan are and answer.

Where is the...

a. school? _____

b. pet shop? _____

c. restaurant? _____

d. supermarket? _____

e. hospital? _____

LANGUAGE TIPS

Os endereços em inglês são escritos da seguinte maneira: 1370 5th Ave, apt. 5b, New York, NY 10118, USA. Geralmente usam-se abreviações para *street* (*St.*), *avenue* (*Ave.*), *road* (*Rd.*) e *apartment* (*apt.*).

2 Read the Central Stadium's address. Is it like your address in Portuguese? Discuss with a classmate.

1450 Main Street

3 Now, go back to the dialog on the previous page and read the directions to get to Central Stadium. Draw a line in the map, helping the kids get there.

A WORD WORK

◀ 1   Listen and repeat the name of the town places.
🔊 31

 museum

 internet café

sports club

 electronic store

 theater

 bakery

 movie theater

 gas station

 drugstore

 bookstore

 laundromat

 bank

◀ 2   What is your favorite place in town? How is it called in English? Talk to your classmates about it.

FIFTY-SEVEN 57

13 Complete the words with the missing vowels. It's possible to write more than one in each gap.

a. sp____rts   cl____b

b. th____t____r

c. b____nk

d. l____ndr____m____t

e. b____k____ry

f. m____v____   th____t____r

g. g____s   st____t____n

h. ____nt____rn____t   c____f____

i. b____kst____r____

j. dr____gst____r____

14 Read the chart and write the directions under the pictures.

| turn left | go down | go straight ahead |
| turn right | go up | walk two blocks |

_____

_____

TIME FOR A GAME

Let's play **Can game** and **Scrambled Words**!

FOCUS ON LANGUAGE

1 Read the sentences below. The words in blue indicate…

> **Allan:** Leo, we are lost. We should ask for directions to get to Central Stadium.
> **Leo:** There is a police officer **next to** the restaurant. Let's talk to him.

a. a quality. ◯   b. a location. ◯   c. a time. ◯

2 Look at the chart and number the sentences according to the prepositions.

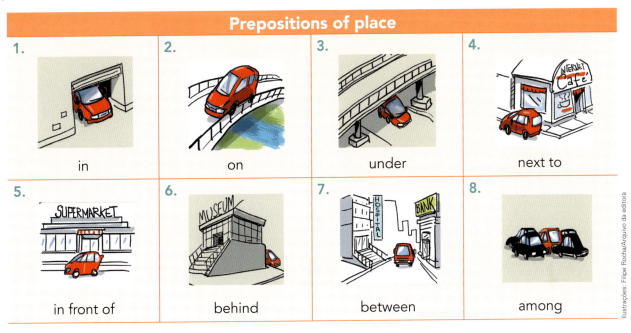

a. ◯ The car is _____ the garage.

b. ◯ The red car is _____ the black ones.

c. ◯ The car is _____ the museum.

d. ◯ The car is _____ the bank and the hospital.

e. ◯ The car is _____ the river bridge.

f. ◯ The car is _____ the viaduct.

g. ◯ The car is _____ the internet café.

h. ◯ The car is _____ the supermarket.

Go to page 155.

13 Complete the sentences using prepositions of place.

a.

b.

c.

d.

e.

f.

a. The museum is _____ the bookstore.

b. The red hair girl is _____ a boy and another girl.

c. The sculpture is _____ the table.

d. The pictures and the sculpture are _____ the museum.

e. The girl is _____ the boy.

f. The boy with green t-shirt is _____ his friends.

14 Now it's your turn! Write two sentences using prepositions of place and illustrate them.

5 Read the comic strip and underline the sentences that indicate orders.

6 Look at the chart and write the commands under the correct pictures.

Imperatives	
Affirmative	**Negative**
Turn right.	**Don't** turn left.
Park your car here.	**Don't** bring your pets here.

 _____

 _____

 _____

 _____

TO LEARN MORE

To ask for the location of a place, you can say:
A: *Where is the Plaza Hotel?*
B: *It's on Main Avenue.*

To ask for the directions to get to a place, you can say:
A: *How do I get to the Plaza Hotel?*
B: *Go down 2ⁿᵈ Street for two blocks and turn left. It's next to the hospital.*

GRAMMAR HELPER

Go to page 155.

7 Look at the map and answer. How do I get to…

a. Bill's Restaurant?
___

b. the theater?
___

c. the Special Drugstore?
___

d. the Plaza Hotel?
___

e. the New Edition Bookstore?
___

f. the internet café?
___

ENGLISH PLUS

To learn and practice giving directions, go to: <www.englishexercises.org/makeagame/viewgame.asp?id=1434>. Accessed on: April 23, 2019.

LISTEN AND SPEAK

1 Listen to some people asking for and giving directions and check the expressions they used.

🔊 32
- ◯ Go up
- ◯ Turn right
- ◯ Go by bus
- ◯ Go to the sports club
- ◯ Turn left
- ◯ Walk two blocks
- ◯ Go straight ahead
- ◯ Go to the theater

2 Listen again, look at the map and write the name of the places that were mentioned.

🔊 33

a. _____

b. _____

c. _____

3 Now, listen one more time and answer **T** (true) or **F** (false).

🔊 34
- a. ◯ People want to visit the shopping mall, the sports club and the supermarket.
- b. ◯ The supermarket is next to the park.
- c. ◯ The sports club is between two houses and an apartment building.
- d. ◯ The shopping mall is on Brodway Avenue.

SIXTY-THREE 63

4 Draw your school's neighborhood map. Then tell your classmate how you get to school every day.

PRONUNCIATION CORNER

1 Listen and act out the jazz chant.

🔊 35 **A:** Is Richard's house near or far?

B: Not too far, not too near.

A: Are you sure?

B: Not so sure... By car you turn right, by bike you turn left...

A: Robert! Tell me, where is it?

B: Near the airport, close to the bakery, next to the bookstore...

A: Not too near, not too far...

B: Sorry, Ray! I'm not sure!

2 Read and say.

🔊 36

| rock | restaurant | are | four | car | airport | road | red |

READ AND WRITE

1 Skim the text and check the correct statements about it.

a. ◯ There are visual representations of information such as graphs and pictures.

b. ◯ Information is explained quickly and clearly.

c. ◯ Visual representations are not used to explain the message.

d. ◯ The text is an infographic.

e. ◯ It presents positive and negative facts about pedestrian safety.

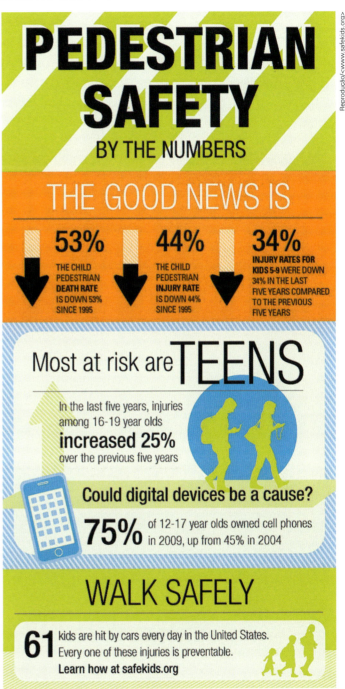

Available at: <https://www.safekids.org/infographic/pedestrian-safety-infographic>. Accessed on: Jan. 16, 2019.

2 Read the sentences and write **T** (true) or **F** (false).

a. ◯ The child pedestrian death rate is down 44% since 1995.

b. ◯ Digital devices are dangerous distractions to pedestrians.

c. ◯ Prevention can avoid being hit by a car.

3 It's your turn to create your own infographic! Follow the steps.

   a. Choose an interesting theme and do some research about it. Take notes in your notebook.
   b. Choose a title to your infographic.
   c. Remember that infographics are visual representations of information. So, you can use graphs, maps, images etc.
   d. Use some imperative sentences in your text and make sure it is concise, clear and well organized.
   e. Write a draft in your notebook and ask the teacher to correct it.
   f. Make all the necessary changes.
   g. In a sheet of paper, glue or draw the visual elements and write a final version.

4 Now, share your infographic with your classmates.

TIPS FOR LIFE

Beware on the streets

1 Read the text and the poster. Then discuss with your classmates: Do you usually pay attention when crossing the street?

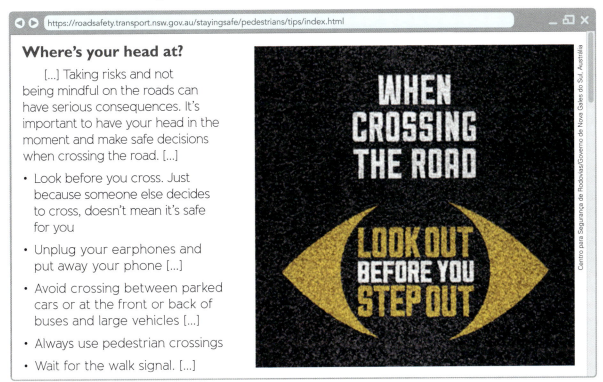

Where's your head at?

[...] Taking risks and not being mindful on the roads can have serious consequences. It's important to have your head in the moment and make safe decisions when crossing the road. [...]

- Look before you cross. Just because someone else decides to cross, doesn't mean it's safe for you
- Unplug your earphones and put away your phone [...]
- Avoid crossing between parked cars or at the front or back of buses and large vehicles [...]
- Always use pedestrian crossings
- Wait for the walk signal. [...]

Available at: <https://roadsafety.transport.nsw.gov.au/stayingsafe/pedestrians/tips/index.html>.
Accessed on: Dec. 21, 2018.

2 Now, choose one of the tips from activity 1 and create a poster about it.

CHECK YOUR PROGRESS	😃	😐	☹️
Places in the city/ directions/address			
Prepositions of place			
Imperative			
Listening			
Speaking			
Reading			
Writing			

REVIEW

UNITS 3 AND 4

1 Help Joshua find the objects in his bedroom. Read and circle the correct prepositions.

a. The smartphone and the tablet are **in/on** the bed.
b. The pens and pencils are **next to/in front of** the computer.
c. The TV is **in front of/between** his bed.
d. The basketball is **on/in** the box.
e. His school books are **under/between** his bed.
f. The clock is **behind/between** the books.
g. The schoolbag is **on/in front of** the chair.
h. The games are **in front of/behind** the DVD player.

2 Look at Joshua's bedroom again and complete the sentences with **there is** or **there are**.

a. _____ a TV set in Joshua's bedroom.
b. _____ five school books in the bedroom.
c. _____ four pens and two pencils in the pencil holder.
d. _____ one bed in Joshua's bedroom.
e. _____ a schoolbag in the room.
f. _____ a computer on the desk.

3 Answer the questions using the verb to be and short answers.

a. Are you listening to music now?
_____

b. Are your mother and father at the supermarket?
_____

c. Is your school big?
_____

d. Is your brother in his bedroom now?
_____

4 Read the directions given and look at the map to find out the name of the places.

a. Go up one block and turn left on Evans Avenue; then go straight ahead two blocks and stop on the third block. It's on your right. _____

b. Go up two blocks and turn left on Lakeshore Road; then go ahead one block and stop on the second block. It's on your right. _____

c. Go up one block and turn left on Evans Avenue; then go straight ahead three blocks and turn right on Oxford Road. Go ahead one block and stop on the second block. It's on your right. _____

Unit 5 ANIMAL WORLD

◖1 What is the animal in the picture? Do you know other animal names in English?

◖2 Read and listen to the dialog. Then act out.

🔊37 **Leo:** Hey, guys! Check out the book I got at the library.

Allan: *Wild animals...* Is it about dinosaurs?

Kitty: No, Allan, dinosaurs are extinct animals. Wild animals live in a natural environment.

Tobby: Look at these tigers, folks! Where are they from?

Carol: They're Bengal tigers, and they are from Asia. They're beautiful!

Leo: Turn the page... Look at this hippo! It's very strong and heavy.

Allan: And the giraffes are very tall and have long necks.

Kitty: I can see an alligator in this picture. It's huge!

Tobby: Yes, they are, and they keep to themselves, unless they feel threatened.

Carol: Look at this picture! There's a sleepy chimpanzee on the tree! Oh, it's so cute!

Leo: My favorite animals are monkeys! They're so funny... Like me!

Allan: Come on, Leo!

◖3 Read the dialog again and match the columns.

a. alligator   ◯ beautiful
b. chimpanzee   ◯ cute
c. giraffe   ◯ funny
d. hippo   ◯ huge
e. monkey   ◯ strong
f. tiger   ◯ tall

THINKING AHEAD

1 Allan decided to learn more about dinosaurs. Read the text to find out what he has learned.

`www.hello!teens.com/dinosaurs`

Dinosaurs

Dinosaurs were animals that lived more than 100 million years ago. Some dinosaurs were more like reptiles while others were more birdlike. There are over seven hundred (700) different species of dinosaurs identified!

We know about dinosaurs from fossils that are found in the ground. From fossils, scientists can recreate whole skeletons of dinosaurs and determine what they were like. Some of these fossils and skeletons can be seen in museums.

Many scientists believe, based on evidence, that dinosaurs went extinct when the Earth was hit by a giant meteorite, which was followed by a massive volcanic eruption. These events sent up dust and dirt into the sky covering up the sun for a long time, causing the death of many plants and animals. Then, without food, dinosaurs died too.

Meet Some Dinosaurs

Name	Diet	Weight	Main Characteristics	Habitat
1. Apatosaurus (scientific name) **Brontosaurus** (popular name)	Plant eater (herbivorous)	50,000 pounds (22,700 kg)	Giant dinosaur: 75 feet long (23 meters) Long neck and tail; small head Quadruped	It probably lived in North America and Mexico
2. Tyrannosaurus Rex	Carnivorous	33,000 pounds (15,000 kg)	Very strong, fast and intelligent Short arms and long legs Strong bite Bipedal	It lived in North America
3. Velociraptor	Carnivorous	30,000 pounds (13,608 kg)	Birdlike dinosaur Covered in feathers Bipedal	Mongolia, China and other parts of Asia

Based on: <www.ducksters.com/animals/apatosaurus.php>; <https://kids.nationalgeographic.com/animals/hubs/dinosaurs-and-prehistoric/>. Accessed on: Jan. 31, 2019.

2 Number the pictures based on the information from the **Meet Some Dinosaurs** chart, in activity 1.

a.

Hedzun Vasyl/Shutterstock

b.

RikoBest/Shutterstock

c.

metha1819/Shutterstock

A WORD WORK

1 Listen and repeat.
🔊 38

| bear | horse | hen | duck | elephant |

    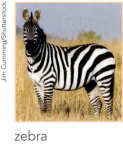

| pig | penguin | starfish | wolf | zebra |

| dog | snake | lion | dolphin | cat |

| rhino | sea turtle | fish | cow | bird |

2 In pairs, classify the animals.

Wild Animals	
Pets	
Farm Animals	
Sea Animals	

SEVENTY-THREE 73

3 Listen and complete the gaps with words from the box.

| fat | long | old | short | small | young | ugly |

a.

The man on the left is **tall** and the man on the right is _____.

b.

The **old** lady is on the left and the _____ girl is on the right.

c.

The cat with a _____ tail is Jim's pet and the cat with a **short** tail is Allan's pet.

d.

The black dog is _____ and the brown dog is **thin**.

e.

The yellow dog house is **new** and the brown dog house is _____.

f.

The green house is **beautiful** and the gray house is _____.

g.

The bus is **big** and the bicycle is _____.

TIME FOR A GAME

Let's play **Bingo** and **Hot Potato**!

FOCUS ON LANGUAGE

1 Answer the questions according to the pictures.

a.

Is the ostrich a small animal?

No, _____

b.

Are sloths fast animals?

No, _____

2 In pairs, read the sentences and circle the correct options.

a. We use **a/an** before words that begin with a vowel sound.

b. We use **a/an** before words that begin with a consonant sound.

3 In pairs, write the words from the box in the correct column. Then, complete the chart.

| ant | eagle | jellyfish | kangaroo | octopus | platypus |

Indefinite articles	
A	AN

SEVENTY-FIVE 75

4 In pairs, read the dialogs and check the correct options to complete the sentence.

The definite article **the** can be used before _____ nouns.

◯ male   ◯ plural   ◯ female   ◯ singular

5 In pairs, write sentences using:

a. the definite article **the** + a male noun in plural.

_____

b. the definite article **the** + a female noun in singular.

_____

6 Complete the sentences with the correct option.

a. It is _____ elephant. (a/an)

b. This is _____ bird. (a/an)

c. _____ giraffes are very tall. (A/The)

Artigos
Antes de substantivos no plural, usamos o artigo definido (*the*). Antes de substantivos no singular, podemos usar artigos definidos ou indefinidos (*the*, *a* ou *an*).

Go to page 156.

7 Read the cartoon and check the correct options.

a. ◯ The cartoon shows that the man can't see well with those glasses.

b. ◯ "**I can** see the same pair of...." is equivalent to "**I am able to** see the same pair of..."

c. ◯ **Can** indicates ability in "**I can** see the same..."

8 Now, read the chart and complete the rules for **can** and **can't**.

Can (ability)	
Affirmative	Parrots can fly.
Interrogative	Can parrots fly?
Negative	Parrots can't swim.

a. In the _____ form, we use **can** + subject + verb.

b. In the _____ form, we use subject + **can** + not + verb.

c. In the _____ form, we use subject + **can** + verb.

9 Read the sentences and fill in the gaps with **can** or **can't**.

a. A shark _____ walk, but it _____ swim fast.

b. A dog _____ fly, but it _____ smell very well.

c. A monkey _____ climb trees and it _____ walk on its legs.

d. A sea turtle _____ sing, but it _____ swim under water.

e. A horse _____ run fast, but it _____ climb trees.

f. A snake _____ walk or run, but it _____ jump.

g. A hen _____ give you eggs, but a rooster _____.

h. A cat _____ climb trees, but it _____ swim under water.

10 In pairs, answer the questions with short answers. Follow the examples.

a. Can cats hunt birds?

Yes, they can.

b. Can cats fly?

No, they can't.

c. Can cats run fast?

_____

d. Can cats jump?

_____

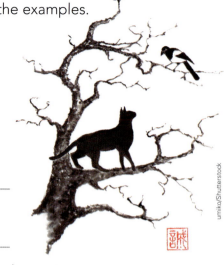

11 Answer about yourself and try to show your ability to your classmates.

a.

Can you sing a song in English?

Yes, I can.

No, I can't.

b.

Can you say the alphabet backwards?

_____

c.

Can you juggle with three erasers?

_____

d.

Can you say a poem?

_____

GRAMMAR HELPER

Go to page 156.

LISTEN AND SPEAK

1 Listen and complete.
🔊 40

koala

chameleon

bear

eagle

ostrich

a. _____ can fly.

b. _____ can hibernate.

c. _____ can run fast.

d. _____ can sleep in a tree.

e. _____ can change into many colors.

2 Listen and write the adjectives you hear.
🔊 41

a.

b.

c.

_____   _____   _____
_____   _____   _____

SEVENTY-NINE 79

3 Talk about the pictures with a classmate. Follow the example.

Giant pandas

Lion and lioness

I can see one giraffe and five zebras in this picture. Giraffes are tall. They are yellow and brown. The zebras are black and white.

PRONUNCIATION CORNER

1 Listen and practice the jazz chant.

🔊 42
- **A:** Is there a mile in a smile?
- **B:** Yes, a long mile in smile!
- **B:** Sssssssssssssssmile… mile!
- **A:** Yes, yes! There is a mile in smile!

- **B:** Is the next station closed?
- **C:** Completely closed, sir!
- **B:** What a situation!
- **C:** Get off at the next station.

2 Listen and say.
🔊 43

| smile | small | snake | station | starfish | speak |

3 List some other words with similar **s + consonant** sound.

_____
_____

ENGLISH PLUS

Para saber mais sobre *giant pandas* e *lions*, assista, respectivamente, aos vídeos <https://www.youtube.com/watch?v=dqT-UlYlg1s> e <https://www.youtube.com/watch?v=zobZd8Mp3sk>. Acesso em: 18 jan. 2019.

READ AND WRITE

1 Read the fact file about great white sharks. Then, check the correct sentences about them.

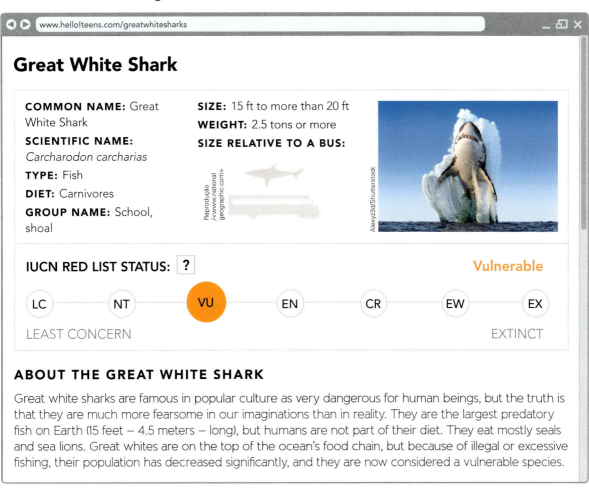

Based on: <https://www.nationalgeographic.com/animals/fish/g/great-white-shark/>.
Accessed on: Jan. 24, 2019.

a. They usually eat…
   ○ people.   ○ other sharks.   ○ seals and sea lions.

b. Great whites are vulnerable because…
   ○ of natural predators.   ○ of human activity.   ○ they are carnivorous.

2 Read the sentences about fact files and write **T** (true) or **F** (false) based on the text in activity 1.

a. ○ A fact file presents information in topics.
b. ○ Fact files don't have any pictures.
c. ○ The information in a fact file is short and precise.
d. ○ An informative paragraph can follow the fact file to give further information on the subject.

3 You are going to write a fact file about an animal. What animal do you want to write about? Why? Tell your classmates.

4 What information can be included in a fact file about animals? Read the items and check the correct options.

- a. ◯ Popular and scientific name of the animal
- b. ◯ Habitat
- c. ◯ Diet
- d. ◯ Detailed and long physical description
- e. ◯ Physical characteristics (size and weight)

5 Write your own animal fact file! You can choose an animal from **Word Work** or another animal you like. Remember: Fact files present short and precise information.

169

a. Do some research before you start writing so you have all the information you need.

b. Choose a picture of the animal to illustrate your fact file.

c. Write a draft paragraph in your notebook with extra information about the animal.

d. Show it to your teacher and make the necessary corrections.

e. Write the final version of the fact file in your book.

TIPS FOR LIFE

Respect and care for animals

1. Look at the picture. Describe what you see.

2. Now, interview someone who has or would like to have a pet.

   a. What pet do you have?
   b. What's his/her name?
   c. How often do you look after your pet?

   ○ I never look after my pet.   ○ Sometimes.   ○ I take care of my pet every day.

   d. Check the tasks that are part of a pet owner's daily routine.

   ○ Feed him/her.
   ○ Replace the water for a fresh and clean bowl 3 or 4 times a day.
   ○ Play time with interactive toys.
   ○ Go to the movies.
   ○ Take him/her outside "to go to the toilet" and exercise.
   ○ Go to parties.
   ○ Play video games.
   ○ Do some training like to fetch, heel, come/recall, sit, stay, lie down.
   ○ Invite him/her to calm down and rest.
   ○ Give him/her love, attention, affection.

   Based on: <www.omlet.co.uk/guide/dogs/daily_care_of_a_dog/a_daily_dog_routine>. Accessed on: Jan. 31, 2019.

CHECK YOUR PROGRESS

	😃	😐	☹
Animals			
Adjectives			
Definite and Indefinite Articles/Can (ability)			
Listening			
Speaking			
Reading			
Writing			

Unit 6: I CAN PLAY BASKETBALL

1 Look at the picture, talk to a classmate and answer.

a. In your opinion, is it important to practice sports? Why?

b. What are the advantages and disadvantages of practicing sports?

2 Read and listen to the dialog. Then act out.

44

Carol: Hey guys, are you ready to go?

Leo: Yes, we are. I'm very excited about the basketball game today.

Kitty: Your team's jersey "The Jaguars" is beautiful, Allan! Is basketball your favorite sport?

Allan: Yes, it is. What's your favorite sport, Kitty?

Kitty: My favorite sport is skateboarding! I love the Brazilian skater Leticia Bufoni.

Allan: Can you skateboard, Kitty?

Kitty: No, I can't, but I can play volleyball. What about you, Jim?

Jim: I love e-sports: playing video games, you know?

Kitty: Look! The Jaguars are waving to their fans. Cool!

Bart: Look, the Raptors are taking their team picture now!

Julie: I am taking a picture of the Raptors now. The referee is whistling! The match is starting!

Bart: Let's cheer to support the Raptors!

Everybody: Go, Raptors!

3 Read the dialog again and answer **T** (true) or **F** (false). Then correct the false statements.

a. ◯ Leo is excited about the volleyball game.

b. ◯ Leticia Bufoni is Kitty's idol.

c. ◯ Julie is taking pictures of the players.

d. ◯ Allan is wearing a Raptors' jersey.

THINKING AHEAD

1 Read the text below.

What Are the Benefits of Playing a Sport for Teens?

Playing sports helps you stay fit. But this is not the only benefit. Here is a quick look at how playing sports can benefit teens.

1. **Social Development:** Playing sports help you grow socially.
2. **Leadership Qualities:** Sports are an excellent exercise to build team spirit and leadership skills.
3. **Long Lasting Friendships:** You may form some very strong bonds that can last a lifetime.
4. **Coach As a Role Model:** A coach teaches you about the importance of discipline in life.
5. **Stamina:** As you play sports, you build your stamina. Sports will help you stay healthy and also increase your mental health and strength.
6. **Time Management:** When you get involved in sports, you also start managing your time better. This means that you can utilize your time productively.

Based on: <www.momjunction.com/articles/benefits-of-playing-sports-for-teens_00329629/#gref>.
Accessed on: Jan. 23, 2019.

2 Choose and write three of the six benefits listed in the text that are the most important to you. Justify your answer.

_____

_____

3 Discuss with a partner.

a. Do you practice any sports? Which ones?

b. How often do you practice sports?

WORD WORK

1 Look at the icons and write the name of the sports using the words from the box. Then listen and repeat.

> basketball   cycling   gymnastics   handball   judo
> canoeing   soccer   swimming   table tennis   tennis
> volleyball   beach volleyball   badminton   athletics

a.
_____

b.
_____

c.
_____

d.
_____

e.
_____

f.
_____

g.
_____

h.
_____

i.
_____

j.
_____

k.
_____

l.
_____

m.
_____

n.
_____

CROSS CULTURAL

No inglês britânico, o futebol é chamado de *football*; já nos Estados Unidos, ele é chamado de *soccer*. Lá, *football* é o que nós chamamos de futebol americano.

2. Read the chart with the verbs and the names of the sports. Then write two more examples to complete it.

do	go	play
(individual or non-team sports or recreational activities)	(movement or you have to go some place to practice it; individual sports)	(competitive sports with teams, rules and competition)
gymnastics	swimming	baseball
judo	cycling	soccer
karate	running/jogging	table tennis
ballet	windsurfing	volleyball
_____	_____	_____
_____	_____	_____

3. Read the definitions and write: What sports are they?

a. A game played on a field between two teams of 11 players each with a round ball. _____

b. A competitive sport in which individuals perform acrobatic feats. _____

c. A sport in which two people fight using their arms and legs, hands and feet, and try to throw each other to the ground. _____

d. The sport of riding a bicycle. _____

e. A game similar to football, played by hitting a ball with your hands instead of your feet. _____

f. A game that is played on a large table where two or four players hit a ball over a net using small, round bats. _____

g. To move through water by moving the body or parts of the body. _____

h. A game played between two or four people on a special playing area that involves hitting a small ball across a central net using a racket. _____

i. A form of volleyball played on sand by teams of two players. _____

Based on: <https://dictionary.cambridge.org/dictionary/english/>. Accessed on: Jan. 23, 2019.

Let's play **Communicative Game** and **Brainstorm**!

FOCUS ON LANGUAGE

1 Look at the pictures, read the sentences and do the activities.

They **are playing** basketball.

She **is skateboarding** at the skate park.

a. What are the words that indicate the actions in the pictures?

b. Check what is true about these sentences.

○ They are about actions that happened in the past.

○ They describe actions that are in progress when speaking.

○ The verb **to be** is used in the sentence structure.

○ There is a main verb ending in -ing.

c. Now underline the correct structure of the Present Continuous.

○ 1. Subject + to be + main verb ending in -ing + complement

○ 2. Subject + main verb + to be ending in -ing + complement

Present Continuous		
Affirmative		
Subject	To be (Present)	Main verb ending in -ing
Paul	is	**playing** volleyball.
Interrogative		
To be (Present)	Subject	Main verb ending in -ing
Is	Paul	**playing** volleyball?
Negative		
Subject	To be (Present + not)	Main verb ending in -ing
Paul	is not (isn't)	**playing** volleyball.

Go to page 156.

2 In pairs, write two sentences using verbs in the Present Continuous.

_____

_____

EIGHTY-NINE 89

3 Read the chart. Then fill in the gaps with the verbs from the box in the Present Continuous and order the dialog sequence.

Spelling rules for *-ing* form	
Regular verbs (walk)	Add *-ing* to the base form (walk**ing**).
Verbs ending in **y** (play, study)	Add *-ing* form after **y** (play**ing**, study**ing**).
Verbs ending in **consonant + e** (dance, practice)	Eliminate the letter **e** and add *-ing* (danc**ing**, practic**ing**).
Verbs ending in **ee** (see)	Add *-ing* to the base form (see**ing**).
Verbs ending in **a vowel + a consonant** (swim)	Double the consonant and add *-ing* (swimm**ing**).
Verbs ending in **a consonant + a vowel + a consonant** (run)	Double the consonant and add *-ing* (runn**ing**).

> do   clean   watch   do   text   practice

○ **Liz:** And your sister, what is she _____ now?

○ **Leo:** He is _____ basketball.

○ **Liz:** You're a good boy, Leo!

○ **Liz:** And you are _____ the yard, I see?

○ **Leo:** He is _____ sports on TV, mom.

○ **Liz:** OK. What about your brother?

○ **Leo:** Yes, I am, mom!

○ **Leo:** She is _____ her friends.

○ **Liz:** What is your father _____, Leo?

GRAMMAR HELPER
Go to page 157.

4 Look at the picture and complete the sentences about Garfield using the Present Continuous.

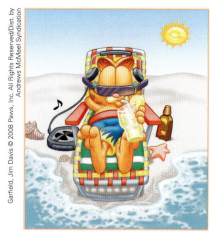

a. Garfield _____ computer games. (play)

b. Garfield _____ . (sunbathe)

c. He _____ a sandwich. (eat)

d. Garfield _____ on the beach. (rest)

e. He _____ on a beach chair. (sit)

f. He _____ with his friends. (talk)

5 Read the chart and complete the short answers.

Present Continuous – Short answers	
Is she listening to music?	Yes, she is. No, she is not (isn't).
Are you chatting with friends?	Yes, _____. No, _____ (I'm not).
Are they skateboarding?	Yes, _____. No, _____ (they aren't).

GRAMMAR HELPER
Go to page 157.

6 Look at the pictures and complete the questions according to their answers. Use the verbs from the box in the Present Continuous.

eat   play   ~~study~~   watch   run   swim

On the beach

1. Where _____
   They are swimming in the sea.

2. _____ the boy _____
   Yes, _____.

What is on TV?

1. _____ sports on TV?
   Yes, _____.

2. Which teams _____ soccer?
   Brazil and England.

At school

1. ____ the teacher _____ a sandwich?
   Yes, _____.

2. What _____ studying?
   We don't know!

7 Read about Fuyumi Sato and write what she **can** or **can't** do. Follow the example.

Name: Fuyumi Sato
Age: 10 years old
Place of birth: Kyoto, Japan
Favorite sport: martial arts (kendo), swimming
Favorite free time activities: origami, fishing
Family: mother, father, older sister
Religion: Buddhist
School: 6th grade

a. Fuyumi can make origami. (make origami)

b. _____. (fish/swim)

c. _____. (practice judo)

d. _____. (practice kendo)

e. _____. (play a musical instrument)

8 Listen and complete the chart and the rules for the ordinal numbers.

46 Fuyumi is in the 6th grade at school. 6th is an ordinal number.

1st	2nd	3rd	4th	5th	6th	7th	8th
first	second	third	fourth	fifth	six___	seventh	eighth
9th	**10th**	**11th**	**12th**	**13th**	**14th**	**15th**	**16th**
nin___	tenth	eleventh	twelfth	thirteen___	fourteenth	fifteenth	sixteenth
17th	**18th**	**19th**	**20th**	**21st**	**22nd**	**23rd**	**24th**
seventeen___	eighteenth	nineteen___	twentieth	twenty-fir___	twenty-seco___	twenty-thi___	twenty-four___
25th	**26th**	**27th**	**30th**	**40th**	**50th**		
twenty-fifth	twenty-sixth	twenty-seventh	thirtieth	fortieth	fiftieth		

a. -st is used with the ordinal number _____.

b. -nd is used with the ordinal number _____.

c. _____ is used with the ordinal numbers fourth, fifth, sixth, seventh, eighth, ninth, tenth.

LISTEN AND SPEAK

1 Read, look at the picture and discuss with a classmate.

> www.hello!teens.com/sports/Marta
>
> **BRAZIL IS NOT A SUPPORTIVE COUNTRY FOR WOMEN'S SOCCER, BUT MARTA IS HELPING TO BREAK THIS OLD RULE**

a. Do you know this woman? Where is she in the picture?

b. In activity 2, you are going to listen to a news article about Marta. What words do you think will complete the gaps? Write them in your notebook.

2 Listen and fill in the gaps.
47

> www.hello!teens.com/sports/Marta
>
> Marta Vieira da Silva is a famous Brazilian _____. She plays for the Orlando Pride, in Miami, for the National Women's Soccer League and she also _____ for the Brazilian National _____. She was born in the small town of Dois Riachos, Alagoas, in Brazil. Marta was named the world's best female soccer player by FIFA, six times already. The UN Women (The United Nations Entity for Gender Equality and the Empowerment of _____) named her Goodwill Ambassador for women and girls in _____. Marta wants to empower and inspire _____ all over the world to challenge gender stereotypes and to fight for what they want. Nowadays, Marta represents women's _____, because she is an outstanding inspiration for girls and women all over the world. She has a powerful story of courage and _____. She is very talented. Her _____ is: "Believe in yourself and trust yourself, because if you don't _____ in yourself, no one else will."

To listen to Marta's message as UN Women's Goodwill Ambassador for women and girls in sports, go to: <www.youtube.com/watch?time_continue=4&v=tV3c3K8Kj70>. Accessed on: Jan. 24, 2019.

NINETY-THREE 93

3 Now, talk to a classmate about Marta's message:

> "Believe in yourself and trust yourself, because if you don't believe in yourself, no one else will."

a. Do you think women can play soccer as well as men? Why?

b. Do you agree with Marta?

c. Do you think Marta is a successful athlete because she believes and trusts herself?

PRONUNCIATION CORNER

1 Listen and act out the tongue twister.
🔊 48

What's the king doing?
The king is running.
What's the queen doing?
The queen is singing.
What's Mary String doing?
She is bringing something pink for the queen,
Bringing something pink for the queen?
Yes, since this morning, she is making something pink for the queen.

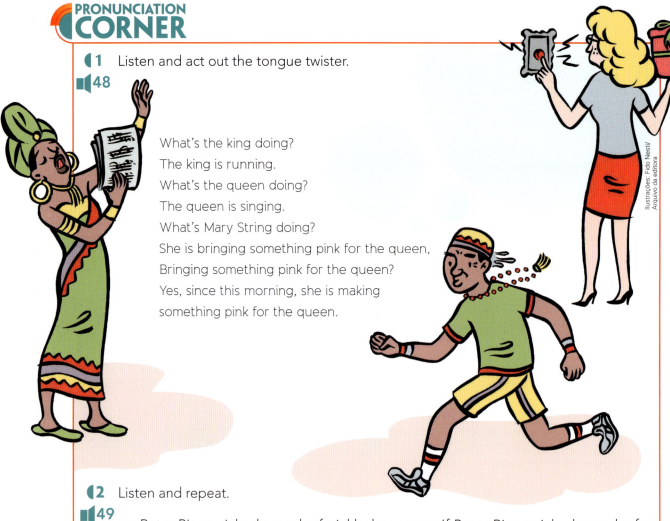

2 Listen and repeat.
🔊 49

a. Peter Piper picked a peck of pickled peppers. If Peter Piper picked a peck of pickled peppers, where's the peck of pickled peppers Peter Piper picked?

b. I scream, you scream, we all scream for ice cream!

c. I saw Susie sitting in a shoeshine shop. Where she sits she shines, and where she shines she sits.

d. Susie's sister sewed socks for soldiers.

e. A proper cup of coffee from a proper copper coffee pot.

READ AND WRITE

1 Read the text below quickly and choose the correct alternative.

This text is…

a. ◯ a fact file. b. ◯ a poster. c. ◯ an online profile.

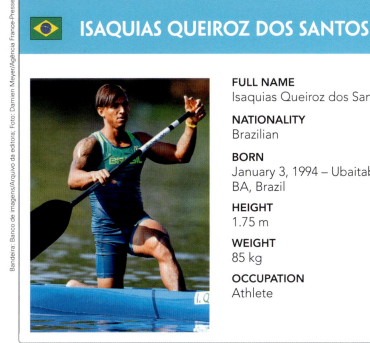

Based on: <www.canoeicf.com/athlete/isaquias-queiroz-dos-santos>.
Accessed on: Jan. 24, 2019.

2 Read the text and check the correct answers.

a. A profile is a
◯ fictional text. ◯ non-fictional text.

b. A profile presents
◯ a person's opinion about a subject. ◯ information about a person's life.

3 Read the text again and answer the questions.

a. What is his full name? _____

b. How old is Isaquias? _____

c. What are his hobbies? _____

d. Who are his idols? _____

4 It's your turn to write a profile.

   a. Choose an athlete or any celebrity that you like.
   b. Search information about the person you chose (full name, date and place of birth, age, nationality, school, family, favorite color, favorite number, favorite food, favorite sport, favorite soccer team, hobbies, pets, favorite subject at school, idols etc.).
   c. Select the information to insert in the profile.
   d. Select a picture to illustrate it.
   e. Write a draft of it in your notebook.
   f. Show it to your teacher and make the necessary corrections.
   g. Then write the final version of the profile in a sheet of paper.

5 Now, share your profile with your classmates. Then prepare the bulletin board to exhibit your profiles.

TIPS FOR LIFE

Fair play

1. Read the questions and discuss them with your classmates.

   a. What is fair play to you?
   b. Why is fair play important in sports?
   c. Give examples of fair play.

2. In groups, create a poster about what fair play means to you.

CHECK YOUR PROGRESS	😀	😐	☹️
Sports			
Ordinal Numbers (1-50)			
Present Continuous			
-ing spelling rules			
Listening			
Speaking			
Reading			
Writing			

REVIEW
UNITS 5 AND 6

1 Write the correct definite (**the**) or indefinite (**a/an**) articles to complete the sentences.

a. Where is _____ cat, Sally?

b. I want to eat _____ apple now. Where can I find one?

c. John is _____ teacher, but he is not our teacher.

d. Melinda has _____ sister and two brothers.

e. _____ Spider-Man movies are very funny.

f. Do you have _____ eraser? Can I borrow it?

2 Read the sentences and complete with **can** or **can't**. Then match the sentences to the pictures.

a. A monkey _____ fly, but it _____ jump and swing from trees.

b. A shark _____ swim fast, but it _____ run.

c. A bear _____ eat fruit, fish and berries, but it _____ fly.

d. A giraffe _____ climb trees, but it _____ eat leaves from tall trees.

13 Look at the icons and write the name of the sports using the words from the box.

> cycling   equestrian   gymnastics   handball   running
> soccer   swimming   tennis   volleyball

_____ _____ _____ _____ _____

_____ _____ _____ _____

14 Circle six verbs in the word search. Then use them to complete the sentences in the Present Continuous.

a. I _____ table tennis with Julian now. (affirmative)

b. John _____ sports on TV. (affirmative)

c. They _____ English. (negative)

d. What _____ Liz _____? (interrogative)

e. We _____ pictures. (negative)

f. _____ she _____ for the Science test? (interrogative)

A	F	I	A	M	E	G	F	H	T	C	K	L	P
S	D	H	G	E	H	A	A	R	E	A	D	H	A
L	F	I	B	X	Q	N	S	J	H	V	C	A	W
B	R	A	Q	I	P	I	P	M	A	M	U	I	A
F	E	M	C	C	L	G	E	P	L	K	F	X	T
B	N	H	D	A	A	E	A	L	M	E	T	U	C
O	S	T	U	D	Y	R	K	K	L	O	P	T	H
L	E	H	P	O	U	I	G	P	A	P	O	I	S
W	X	A	P	L	E	Y	S	D	E	I	P	O	K
D	E	S	D	Q	X	N	E	T	A	K	E	X	U
I	B	X	C	C	F	G	L	J	U	T	D	M	J

Unit 7
YOU ARE WHAT YOU EAT

1. Look at the picture. In pairs, discuss: What is this picture about?

2. Read and listen to the dialog. Then act out. 🔊 50

John: Leo, let's check our shopping list… We need some fruit, a carton of milk, a box of cereal, a carton of orange juice…

Leo: Are these organic apples okay, dad?

John: Yes, they are. Now, a carton of orange juice.

Leo: It is here, but this carton of orange juice is too expensive!

John: How much is it, son?

Leo: It's six dollars each.

John: So, let's take this other one. It costs only three dollars each.

Leo: Yes, dad. And what about those frozen hamburgers? Let's take six of them. They only cost two dollars each.

John: No, Leo! It's not a good idea.

Leo: Why not?

John: Because they're not healthy.

Leo: OK, dad. Look! A special offer for a pack of cereal boxes. Only four dollars.

John: How many boxes are there in each pack?

Leo: There are three boxes in each pack.

John: OK. Let's take one pack.

Leo: What else, dad?

John: A bunch of carrots, a dozen eggs, a pound of cherries and a pound of tomatoes…

Leo: Okay!

3. Read and choose the correct answers.

a. John and Leo are at the
   ○ shopping mall.   ○ supermarket.

b. John wants to
   ○ buy healthy food.   ○ buy junk food.

THINKING AHEAD

1 🔊 51 Read the numbers. Then listen and complete the missing ones.

1	one	10	ten	19	nineteen	80	_____
2	two	11	eleven	20	_____	90	ninety
3	_____	12	twelve	21	twenty-one	100	one hundred
4	four	13	_____	22	_____	101	one hundred and one
5	_____	14	fourteen	30	thirty	200	two hundred
6	six	15	fifteen	40	_____	300	_____
7	seven	16	sixteen	50	fifty	1,000	one thousand
8	_____	17	seventeen	60	sixty	2,000	two thousand
9	nine	18	eighteen	70	seventy	3,000	_____ thousand

TO LEARN MORE

A separação dos números quando atingem a casa do milhar em inglês é marcada pela vírgula, diferentemente do que ocorre em português, no qual se usa ponto. Ex.: 1,500.

2 🔊 52 Listen to the dialogs and write the food prices.

a.    b.    c.   d.

_____   _____   _____   _____

LANGUAGE TIPS

Na linguagem cotidiana, pode-se dizer os preços de modo mais informal. Por exemplo, para $1,40, em vez de *It's one dollar and forty cents*, podemos dizer apenas *It's one forty*.

WORD WORK

1 Listen and repeat.

To make a delicious fruit salad

Vegetables to prepare a salad or a special soup

Dairy products for a healthy breakfast

2 Complete the definitions below by writing **junk food** or **healthy food**. Then identify the pictures as healthy food (**HF**) or junk food (**JF**).

a. _____ is not good for our health because it contains high amounts of salt, fat or sugar, it's high in calories, but low in nutritional content and vitamins.

b. _____ is any food considered to be "good" for you, especially high in fiber, natural vitamins, fructose etc. Examples: apples, beans, carrots, cranberry juice, fish, garlic, ginger, nuts, oats, olive oil, soy foods, tea, yogurt.

3 Read the words from the box below. In pairs, look up for their translation in a bilingual dictionary. Follow the instructions.

> garlic   oats   nuts   soy

a. If the dictionary is printed, search the words following the alphabetical order.

b. If it is an online dictionary, access it on a cell phone, computer, tablet or any other electronic device connected to the internet. Write the word searched in the search field and press enter to see the translation.

c. Write the translations in your notebook and share with your classmates and teacher.

4 Write examples of food you love, like, and dislike. Use a dictionary to help you if necessary.

Love	Like	Dislike

TIME FOR A GAME

Let's play **Hangman** and **What's Missing**!

FOCUS ON LANGUAGE

1. Go back to the dialog on page 101. Find two examples of food in the singular form and two in the plural form and write them below.

_____

_____

2. Based on the examples from the dialog, check the correct option.

   ◯ There are different rules to form the plural with different word ending.

   ◯ The rules and the word endings to form the plural are always the same.

3. Now, look at the plural forms in the chart and complete the sentences.

Regular plural	
+ s	**y → ies**
orange – orange**s**	bab**y** – bab**ies**
hamburger – hamburger**s**	cherr**y** – cherr**ies**
banana – banana**s**	strawberr**y** – strawberr**ies**
+ es	**f/fe → ves**
sandwi**ch** – sandwich**es**	wol**f** – wol**ves**
di**sh** – dish**es**	lea**f** – lea**ves**
tomat**o** – tomato**es**	kni**fe** – kni**ves**
bo**x** – box**es**	li**fe** – li**ves**

Irregular plural	
child – children	mouse – mice
man – men	foot – feet
woman – women	

Go to page 158.

a. The plural form of most nouns is created by adding the letter _____ to the end.

b. The plural form of nouns ending in a **consonant + y** requires _____ to the end of the word.

c. Words ending in **ch**, **sh**, **x**, **o**, **ss** require _____ ending to form the plural.

d. Words ending in **f** or **fe** require _____ ending to form the plural.

4. Write the singular or plural form of the words.

Singular	Plural
apple	apples
woman	
potato	

Singular	Plural
child	children
	cherries
knife	

5 Look at the pictures and read the recipe. Then, write the ingredients and their quantities according to the pictures.

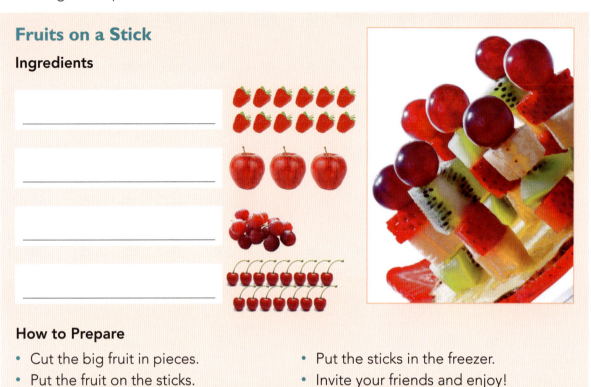

Fruits on a Stick

Ingredients

_____

_____

_____

_____

How to Prepare

- Cut the big fruit in pieces.
- Put the fruit on the sticks.
- Put the sticks in the freezer.
- Invite your friends and enjoy!

6 Read the sentences, look at the pictures and circle the correct answer from the options in bold.

a. The demonstrative pronoun **this/that** is used to indicate people, animals and objects which are near the speaker.

b. The demonstrative pronoun **this/that** is used to indicate people, animals and objects which are far from the speaker.

c. The plural for "this" is **these/those**.

d. The plural for "that" is **these/those**.

GRAMMAR HELPER

Go to page 158.

17 Complete the speech bubbles with **this**, **that**, **these** or **those**.

_____ ARE APPLES AND _____ IS A PINEAPPLE.

_____ IS A BANANA AND _____ ARE ORANGES.

18 Write questions with the words in the same color.

those	that	a piece of	Are	Are	Is	a
those	?	Is	cheddar cheese	diet	?	purple
?	grapes	green	tomatoes	this	?	yogurt

a.

_____
No, it isn't. It's a piece of Italian parmesan cheese.

b.

_____
Yes, they are.

c.

_____
Yes, it is.

d.

_____
No, they aren't. They are red.

9 Read the chart, then write sentences in the Simple Present.

Simple Present				
Affirmative	I, You, We, You, They	eat	healthy food.	
Interrogative	Do	I, you, we, you, they	eat	healthy food?
Negative	I, You, We, You, They	don't (do not)	eat	healthy food.

a. affirmative

_____

b. negative

_____

c. interrogative

_____

10 Read the chart and the questions below. Then underline the correct answers based on your own experiences and routines.

Short Answers	
Do they eat healthy food?	
Affirmative	Yes, they do.
Negative	No, they don't.

a. Do you eat junk food?

Yes, I do./No, I don't.

b. Do you and your parents eat salad every day?

Yes, we do./No, we don't.

c. Do your parents eat meat?

Yes, they do./No, they don't.

d. Do you eat fruit every day?

Yes, I do./No, I don't.

e. Do you usually drink soda with your meals?

Yes, I do./No, I don't.

f. On the weekends, do you go out to eat?

Yes, I do./No, I don't.

GRAMMAR HELPER

Go to page 159.

LISTEN AND SPEAK

1 Go back to page 108 and list the examples of healthy food presented in activity 10.

_____

2 Which of the examples above is your favorite and why? Share ideas with your classmates.

3 Listen to a restaurant chef talking about the ingredients he uses in a healthy recipe. Complete the ingredients list with the correct piece of information.

Ingredients	Quantity	How to use
oranges	_____	peeled and sliced
strawberries	_____	sliced
apple	one	_____ _____
_____	_____	peeled and cut into half inch cubs

LANGUAGE TIPS

The word **veggie** is an informal way of referring to a vegetable in American English. In British English it refers to a vegetarian person.

4 Now, listen to an interview in which a famous nutrologist doctor talks about healthy food
🔊 55 and healthy life habits. Write **T** (true) or **F** (false).

a. ◯ It's not necessary to drink water.

b. ◯ Food gives us energy.

c. ◯ It's important to eat a variety of colorful food.

d. ◯ Doctors tell us the best food is junk food.

e. ◯ Lean meat, fish, eggs and milk are good for your health.

5 Kitty and Sayuri are playing a fun game with food names. Listen and check the name of
🔊 56 the game and the fruit mentioned.

a. ◯ What's the picture?

b. ◯ Guessing game

c. ◯ Hot potato

d. ◯ Orange

6 Now, in pairs, play the game with a classmate.

PRONUNCIATION CORNER

1 Listen and say the tongue twister.
🔊 57
A: Go shopping!

B: Choose some cheese.

A: Choose some cherries.

B: Cheap cheese,
cheap cherries.

A: Cherries? Cheese?
Cheese? Cherries?

B: Don't forget! Pay in cash!

A: Cash or check?
Check or cash?

D: Cash. Pay in cash, please!

2 Listen and circle the words you hear with **ch** sound and underline the words with **sh**
🔊 58 sound.

| shopping cherry cheese cash check choose cheap fish |

READ AND WRITE

1 Read the flyer below. Reflect on the questions that follow and choose the correct answers.

Available at: <https://flyers.smartcanucks.ca/canada/family-foods-flyer-june-1-to-7/single/>.
Accessed on: Feb. 2, 2019.

a. What is the purpose of using flyer design? It's to attract the audience and promote a

○ supermarket.

○ menu from a restaurant.

b. What is the target audience of this flyer?

○ Professional cooks.

○ Customers that live near the supermarket.

2 Underline some characteristics of the flyer from activity 1.

   a. appealing pictures
   b. expiration date of the products
   c. product's name
   d. relevant information such as prices, discounts, and webpage

3 Where are the supermarket flyers probably distributed?

_____

_____

4 Do you think that a flyer is a good way to promote products, stores and services? Why (not)?

_____

5 Which products in this flyer would you be interested in? Why?

_____

6 Now, imagine you own a store and want to promote some services or products. Create a
173 special flyer to do this in your notebook. Follow the instructions.

   a. Choose a creative name to your store and decide what you are going to sell there.
   b. Collect attractive images to catch the attention of your target audience.
   c. Develop a creative flyer design.
   d. Offer relevant and objective information, such as address, phone number, website, prices, discounts etc.
   e. Write a draft in the blank space below, show it to your teacher and make all the necessary adjustments.
   f. Write a final version of your flyer on a separate sheet of paper.
   g. Show your flyer to your classmates and explain it.
   h. Finally, vote for the most creative flyer.

TIPS FOR LIFE

Healthy habits

1 Read the text in pairs and answer.

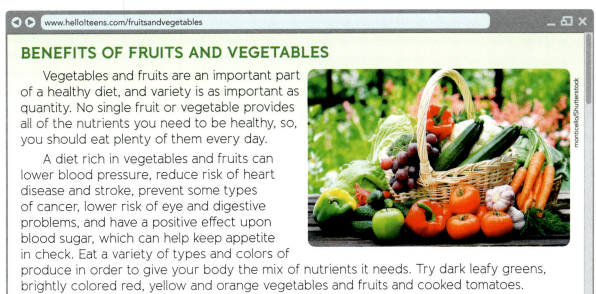

BENEFITS OF FRUITS AND VEGETABLES

Vegetables and fruits are an important part of a healthy diet, and variety is as important as quantity. No single fruit or vegetable provides all of the nutrients you need to be healthy, so, you should eat plenty of them every day.

A diet rich in vegetables and fruits can lower blood pressure, reduce risk of heart disease and stroke, prevent some types of cancer, lower risk of eye and digestive problems, and have a positive effect upon blood sugar, which can help keep appetite in check. Eat a variety of types and colors of produce in order to give your body the mix of nutrients it needs. Try dark leafy greens, brightly colored red, yellow and orange vegetables and fruits and cooked tomatoes.

Based on: <www.hsph.harvard.edu/nutritionsource/what-should-you-eat/vegetables-and-fruits/>.
Accessed on: Jan. 14, 2019.

a. Does the text recommend we eat a variety of fruits every day? Why (not)?

_____

_____

2 Share your opinion about the healthy habits mentioned in the text above with your teacher and classmates.

CHECK YOUR PROGRESS	😃	😐	🙁
Food and drinks			
Regular and Irregular plural forms			
Simple Present			
Demonstrative Pronouns			
Listening			
Speaking			
Reading			
Writing			

Unit 8 — LET'S GO CAMPING!

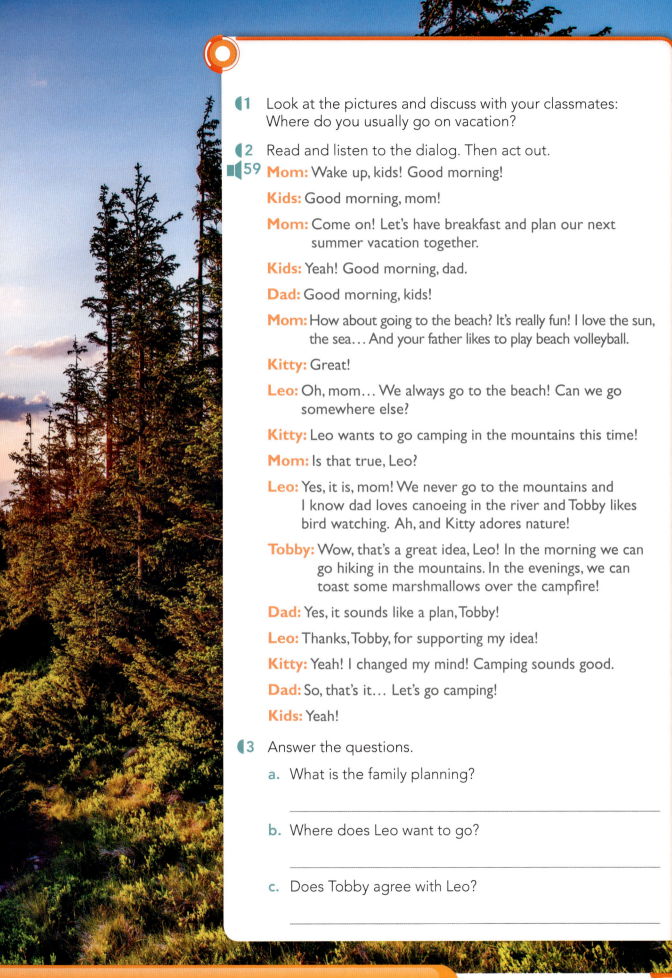

◀1 Look at the pictures and discuss with your classmates: Where do you usually go on vacation?

◀2 Read and listen to the dialog. Then act out.

🔊59 **Mom:** Wake up, kids! Good morning!

Kids: Good morning, mom!

Mom: Come on! Let's have breakfast and plan our next summer vacation together.

Kids: Yeah! Good morning, dad.

Dad: Good morning, kids!

Mom: How about going to the beach? It's really fun! I love the sun, the sea… And your father likes to play beach volleyball.

Kitty: Great!

Leo: Oh, mom… We always go to the beach! Can we go somewhere else?

Kitty: Leo wants to go camping in the mountains this time!

Mom: Is that true, Leo?

Leo: Yes, it is, mom! We never go to the mountains and I know dad loves canoeing in the river and Tobby likes bird watching. Ah, and Kitty adores nature!

Tobby: Wow, that's a great idea, Leo! In the morning we can go hiking in the mountains. In the evenings, we can toast some marshmallows over the campfire!

Dad: Yes, it sounds like a plan, Tobby!

Leo: Thanks, Tobby, for supporting my idea!

Kitty: Yeah! I changed my mind! Camping sounds good.

Dad: So, that's it… Let's go camping!

Kids: Yeah!

◀3 Answer the questions.

a. What is the family planning?

_____

b. Where does Leo want to go?

_____

c. Does Tobby agree with Leo?

_____

THINKING AHEAD

1 Read the Bell's Campground Routine program. Are these activities the same as your daily activities? Talk to a classmate.

Bell's Campground Routine

6:30 a.m. Time to wake up	12:30 a.m. Have lunch
7:00 a.m. Have breakfast	6:00 p.m. Shower time
10:00 a.m. Eat a snack and have a break	7:00 p.m. Have dinner
	10:00 p.m. Time to go to bed

2 Look at the activities the Bell's Campground is offering today. In your opinion, what are the most interesting activities to do? Why? Talk to a classmate.

Today's Activities – Saturday 7th, 2019

8:00 a.m. fishing
9:00 a.m. swimming
10:30 a.m. canoeing
2:00 p.m. mountain biking
3:30 p.m. bird watching
4:00 p.m. go hiking
5:00 p.m. horseback riding
8:00 p.m. roasting marshmallows and singing

3 Write and say. What are the activities you usually do in your free time?

My activities	My friend's activities

A WORD WORK

1. Look at the picture and identify the camping items. Listen and repeat the words.
🔊 60

2 You are packing to go to a campground next weekend. Write the name of six essential objects and clothes to take with you. Work in pairs.

Objects	Clothes
_____	_____
_____	_____
_____	_____
_____	_____
_____	_____
_____	_____

3 Look at the picture and answer: Where is the family going to? What kind of car is this?

CROSS CULTURAL

Nos Estados Unidos, é comum as pessoas viajarem em *motor homes*. Já no Brasil, encontrar um veículo desses na estrada é raro. A cultura de fazer turismo a bordo de um *motor home* é antiga nos Estados Unidos, tanto que no país há milhares de *campgrounds* com estrutura para recebê-los.

TIME FOR A GAME

Let's play **Stop** and **Word list**!

FOCUS ON LANGUAGE

1. Read the sentences below. The words in blue indicate…

   > **Leo:** Yes, it is, mom! We never go to the mountains and I know dad loves canoeing in the river and Tobby likes bird watching. Ah, and Kitty adores nature!

   a. ◯ verbs in the plural. b. ◯ nouns in the plural. c. ◯ 3rd person singular verbs.

2. Read and complete the chart.

   | Verbs ending in consonant + y | Verbs ending in s, z, x, o, sh, ch | Most verbs |

3rd Person Singular (He/She/It) – Spelling Rules	
Verb + s	buy – buys
_____	love – love_____
Verb + es	watch – watches
_____	kiss – kiss_____
Verb -y → ies	fly – flies
_____	carry – carr_____

3. Write the 3rd person singular of the verbs from the box. Go back to the chart in activity 2 if necessary.

   | clean | go | hurry | study | watch | work |

-s	-es	-ies
_____	_____	_____
_____	_____	_____

4. Complete the sentences with some of the verbs from activity 3.

   a. Paul _____ to Green Mountains Camping every year.

   b. My sister _____ Computer Science.

   c. My cousin Miguel _____ sports on TV on the weekends.

   d. Bob's uncle _____ at the camping site. He _____ the kitchen.

5 Read the chart and do the activities.

Simple Present – 3rd Person Singular			
Affirmative	He/She/It	drink**s**	water.
Interrogative	**Does**	he/she/it	drink water?
Negative	He/She/It	do**esn**'t (does not)	drink water.

a. Write the rule for the interrogative and negative forms.

_____

_____

b. Now, write two affirmative sentences in the Simple Present in a sheet of paper. Then ask a classmate to write them into the interrogative and negative forms.

6 Read the chart and answer the questions.

Short Answers – 3rd Person Singular	
Patti play**s** the guitar. **Does** Patti play the guitar well?	
Affirmative	Yes, she **does**.
Negative	No, she **doesn't**.

a. Does anyone in your family swim well? Who?

_____

b. Does your best friend play soccer?

_____

c. Does your neighbor go kayaking?

_____

d. Does your classmate usually go camping with you?

_____

7 Read the text and complete the questions with **do**, **does**, **don't** or **doesn't**.

> Barbara and Charles are P.E. teachers. They live in Boston, in the United States. Charles works at a public school in the mornings and Barbara works at a private school in the afternoons. They teach Elementary and Junior High School students. Sometimes, Charles and Barbara organize competitions among their students.

a. What _____ Charles and Barbara do? They are P.E. teachers.

b. Where _____ Barbara work? She works at a private school.

c. _____ Charles teach Math in the mornings? No, he _____.

d. _____ Charles and Barbara practice sports with their students? No, they _____.

GRAMMAR HELPER

Go to page 159.

8 Read the sentences below. What do the words in blue indicate?

> **Leo:** Oh, mom… We always go to the beach! Can we go somewhere else! […]
>
> **Leo:** Yes, it is, mom! We never go to the mountains and I know dad loves canoeing in the river […]

a. ○ Love for nature and the beach.

b. ○ Frequency they go to the mountains and to the beach.

c. ○ What they do at the beach and mountains.

9 Read the chart. Then unscramble the questions and answer them with the given adverb of frequency. Follow the example.

Adverbs of Frequency	
Always	100%
Usually	70%
Sometimes	50%
Rarely	20%
Never	0%

a. you/go to the mountains/? (never)

   When do you go to the mountains?
   I never go to the mountains.

b. you and your family/go camping/? (often)

   _____

   _____

c. Jim and Carol/play tug of war with their friends/? (sometimes)

   _____

   _____

d. Carol and Kitty/play piggyback at school/? (always)

   _____

   _____

10 Write sentences about yourself using Adverbs of Frequency. Follow the example.

a. I __always__ go to the beach.

b. I _____ do my homework.

c. I _____ eat salad.

d. I _____ play soccer.

e. I _____ watch TV until late at night.

11 Read the text and answer the questions.

a. What is the name of the event?
_____

b. What is the date of the event?
_____

c. Where is it?
_____

d. What are the activities?
_____
_____
_____

e. Is there a contact number?
_____

The dates (in American English)
- We use ordinal numbers to write dates.
- Months are written with capital letters: January, February etc.
- The years are normally divided into two parts (the first two digits and the last two): 2021 is divided into 20 and 21 so you would say: twenty, twenty-one.

12 Read the chart and write dates in full.

Written English	Spoken English	The order of numbers	When the month is written, you use a comma if it is followed by a year
February 5	February fifth	2/5/2021	February 5, 2021.

a. 08/31/1964:
_____

b. 12/11/2008:
_____

c. 5/23/2010:
_____

d. 1/22/2019:
_____

LISTEN AND SPEAK

1. Read the activities below and check the ones you think Jack, Andrea and Susan can do on their camping trip to the mountains.

   ○ beach volleyball
   ○ fish in the lake
   ○ judo
   ○ sing and dance
   ○ horseback riding
   ○ hike
   ○ watch movies
   ○ cook dinner

2. Jack, Andrea and Susan are ready to go camping and they are planning their activities. Listen to their conversation and write **T** (true) or **F** (false). 🔊 61

   a. ○ Jack, Andrea and Susan are going to a camping site.
   b. ○ Breakfast is served at 8 a.m.
   c. ○ There are many activities as fishing, swimming and horseback riding.
   d. ○ Jack can take his violin to camp.

3. Listen to the audio again and check the correct answers. 🔊 62

   a. Who loves to go fishing?
      ○ Andrea does.
      ○ Jack does.
      ○ Susan does.

   b. The evening activities are:
      ○ horseback riding.
      ○ singing, dancing and roasting marshmallows.
      ○ fishing and swimming.

   c. At 4:00 p.m., the kids can...
      ○ go hiking or swimming.
      ○ have a snack by the lake.
      ○ go hiking or horseback riding.

ONE HUNDRED AND TWENTY-THREE 123

d. What time is dinner served at the camp?
- ○ At 6:30 p.m.
- ○ At 7:30 p.m.
- ○ At 8:30 a.m.

4 What activities from the camping site would you like to do? Why? Share your answers with a classmate.

_____
_____
_____
_____

5 Imagine you are on a campground and talk to a classmate about your routine there. Use the questions below to guide your conversation:

- What is the name of the campground?
- How far is it from your home?
- What time do you wake up/have lunch/have dinner/go to bed there?
- What are the camping special activities?

PRONUNCIATION CORNER

1 Listen and act out the jazz chant.

🔊 63

A: Class, this is the Math teacher.

B: Pardon, what's your name?

C: Ms. Smith. Ms. Dorothy Smith.

B. Welcome, Ms. Smith!

C: Thank you, class!

B: This is for you, Ms. Smith.

C: Thanks, class! Thanks a lot!

2 Listen and circle the word you hear.

🔊 64

a. tank/thank
b. three/tree
c. mouth/mouse
d. day/they
e. thin/sin

READ AND WRITE

1 Read the text quickly and choose the correct answers.

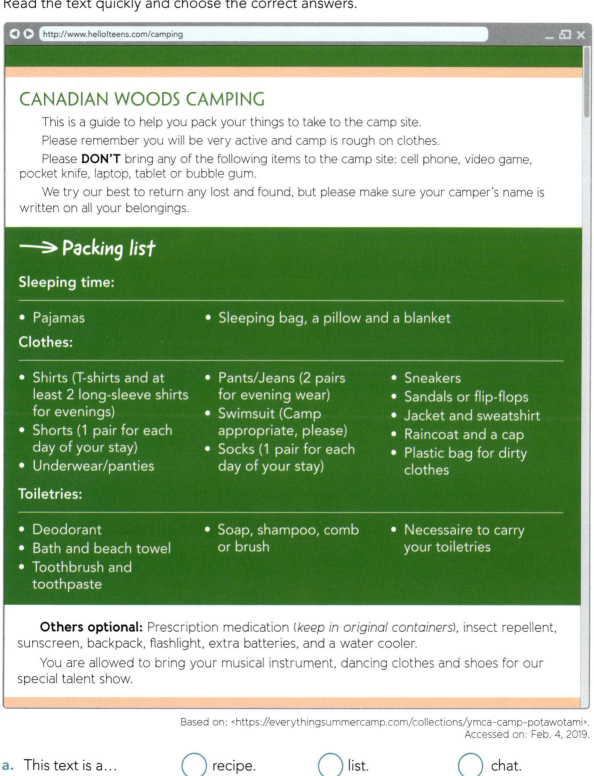

CANADIAN WOODS CAMPING

This is a guide to help you pack your things to take to the camp site.

Please remember you will be very active and camp is rough on clothes.

Please **DON'T** bring any of the following items to the camp site: cell phone, video game, pocket knife, laptop, tablet or bubble gum.

We try our best to return any lost and found, but please make sure your camper's name is written on all your belongings.

→ Packing list

Sleeping time:

- Pajamas
- Sleeping bag, a pillow and a blanket

Clothes:

- Shirts (T-shirts and at least 2 long-sleeve shirts for evenings)
- Shorts (1 pair for each day of your stay)
- Underwear/panties
- Pants/Jeans (2 pairs for evening wear)
- Swimsuit (Camp appropriate, please)
- Socks (1 pair for each day of your stay)
- Sneakers
- Sandals or flip-flops
- Jacket and sweatshirt
- Raincoat and a cap
- Plastic bag for dirty clothes

Toiletries:

- Deodorant
- Bath and beach towel
- Toothbrush and toothpaste
- Soap, shampoo, comb or brush
- Necessaire to carry your toiletries

Others optional: Prescription medication (*keep in original containers*), insect repellent, sunscreen, backpack, flashlight, extra batteries, and a water cooler.

You are allowed to bring your musical instrument, dancing clothes and shoes for our special talent show.

Based on: <https://everythingsummercamp.com/collections/ymca-camp-potawotami>.
Accessed on: Feb. 4, 2019.

a. This text is a… ◯ recipe. ◯ list. ◯ chat.

b. The text is about a… ◯ shopping list for groceries. ◯ mobile phone address list. ◯ packing list for camping.

2 Read and write **T** (true) or **F** (false).

a. ◯ The organizers recommend bringing expensive clothing for camp.
b. ◯ Cell phone and pocket knife are not allowed in the camp site.
c. ◯ Flashlight and sunscreen are optional items.
d. ◯ Backpack is not an optional item.
e. ◯ For hiking, campers should bring boots.
f. ◯ Campers can bring musical instruments and dance clothes for the talent show.

3 Answer the following questions.

a. Is it necessary to bring food for camping? _____

b. Is it necessary to name all the items to take to the camping site? _____

c. What is prohibited to bring to the camp site? _____
_____

4 Suppose you are going to a camping site with your family. Create your own packing list.

a. Choose the items you need to take to the camping trip and list them. Use a dictionary if necessary.
b. Write a draft of the list in your book.
c. Show it to your teacher and make the necessary corrections.
d. Write the final version of the packing list in a sheet of paper.
e. You and your classmates can prepare a bulletin board to show your packing lists.

TIPS FOR LIFE

Respect rules: good camping manners

1. Read the sentences, discuss the camping manners with a classmate and check the ones you agree with.

   - ◯ Greet each other.
   - ◯ Keep the campground clean.
   - ◯ Leave no trace of your visit.
   - ◯ Pick up your trash.
   - ◯ Be friendly to other campers.
   - ◯ Be respectful of nature.
   - ◯ Respect quiet hours.
   - ◯ Respect the schedule.
   - ◯ Respect the rules of the camp.
   - ◯ Respect wildlife.

2. Now, write two more good camping manners.

   _____

   _____

❌ CHECK YOUR PROGRESS	😃	😐	🙁
Daily routines/activities/camping items			
Simple Present – 3rd person singular			
Adverbs of frequency/dates			
Listening			
Speaking			
Reading			
Writing			

REVIEW

UNITS 7 AND 8

1 Write the words from the box into their correct plural column.

| apple | banana | box | carrot | cherry | egg | grape | half | hamburger |
| mango | orange | peach | potato | strawberry | tomato | vegetable |

-s	-ies	-es	-ves

2 Rewrite the sentences and change the underlined words into the plural form. Make the necessary adjustments.

a. This <u>sandwich</u> is in the <u>box</u>.
_____

b. The <u>computer</u> at school is new.
_____

c. That is my English <u>book</u> on the <u>bed</u>.
_____

d. Jimmy has an <u>apple</u> for break time.
_____

e. I can see a <u>fish</u> in the bowl.
_____

3 Read the sentences and underline the correct forms that complete them.

a. I **don't**/doesn't go to the beach every day.

b. What **does**/do Leo do on Saturdays?

c. My friend study/**studies** in a school near the Green Camp site.

d. Mary serve/**serves** people in a restaurant on the beach.

e. Does your mother **like**/likes to go camping?

f. Does/**Do** you have a flashlight?

g. My father **likes**/like to teach at our school.

4 Complete the sentences using **always**, **usually**, **sometimes**, **rarely** or **never** and the correct form of the verb in parentheses.

a. I always make (make) my bed on weekdays.

b. My brother _____ (listen) to rock music.

c. I _____ (go) to the movies with my best friends.

d. I _____ (eat) fruits and vegetables.

e. My sister _____ (help) me with my Math homework.

f. I _____ (play) computer games before dinner.

g. On the weekends, I _____ (eat) pancakes with honey and fruits for breakfast.

5 Write the numbers.

a. 100 – _____

b. 1,000 – _____

c. 1,000,000 – _____

d. 300 – _____

e. 2,000 – _____

f. 3,000,000 – _____

EXTRA PRACTICE

UNITS 1 AND 2

1 Read the infographic and check the correct answer. What is it about?

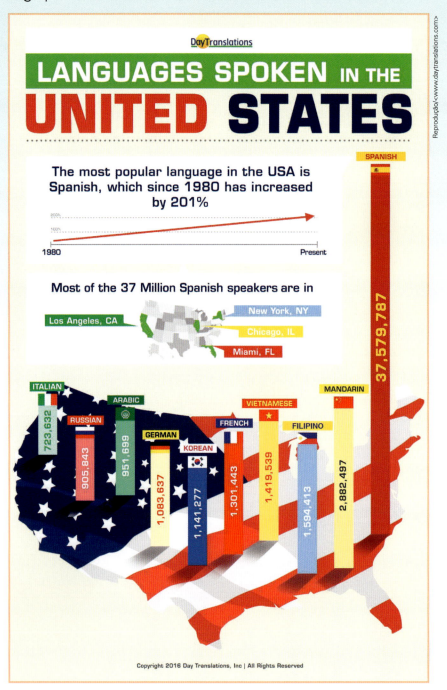

a. ◯ It is about the most popular languages in the world.
b. ◯ It is about the most popular official languages in the world.
c. ◯ It is about the most popular languages in the United States.

2 Read the infographic from activity 1 and answer.

a. Number 1 language in the USA: _____

b. Number 2 language in the USA: _____

c. Number 3 language in the USA: _____

3 Read the infographic once again and choose the correct answers.

a. How many people speak Spanish in the USA?
   ◯ More than 37 million people.
   ◯ More than 201 million people.

b. What language is spoken by less than 900,000 people?
   ◯ Italian
   ◯ Russian

c. Where in the USA is Spanish mostly spoken?
   ◯ In the north side of the country.
   ◯ In the east side of the country.

4 Match the languages to the countries in which they are spoken.

a. Arabic		◯ Germany
b. French		◯ Russia
c. German		◯ China
d. Italian		◯ Vietnam
e. Korean		◯ Spain, Argentina, Bolivia etc.
f. Mandarin		◯ Italy
g. Filipino		◯ France, Ivory Coast, Senegal etc.
h. Russian		◯ The Philippines
i. Spanish		◯ Tunisia, Egypt, Syria etc.
j. Vietnamese		◯ North Korea and South Korea

5 What are the languages spoken in your country? Talk to your classmates and teacher.

EXTRA PRACTICE

UNITS 3 AND 4

1 Read the advertisement below and answer. What is it advertising?

- a. ◯ Apartments for rent.
- b. ◯ Apartments for sale.
- c. ◯ Furniture for sale.

2 Match the abbreviations to the corresponding words.

a. mo ◯ not available
b. sq ft ◯ monthly
c. bdrm ◯ bedroom
d. bth ◯ square feet
e. N/A ◯ bathroom

3 Read the advertisement again and answer **T** (true) or **F** (false).

a. ◯ There is only one 3-bedroom apartment layout.
b. ◯ There aren't any apartments available for rent.
c. ◯ The 2-bedroom apartments have 1 bathroom.
d. ◯ The 1-bedroom apartments have 1,267 square feet.
e. ◯ Dogs are allowed in these apartments.

4 Read the advertisement again. Then check the items that are available in the apartments.

a.
b.
c.
d.
e.
f.
g.
h.
i.

5 How would you advertise the house of your dreams?

ONE HUNDRED AND THIRTY-THREE **133**

EXTRA PRACTICE

UNITS 5 AND 6

1 Read the article below. What is it about?

www.hello!teens.com/nature

JAYDON COLIN-MICHAEL NOLAN JUNE 21, 2016

See different colors
Birds have the fascinating ability to see colors which are invisible to humans. This is due to the extra color cones in their retina which are sensitive to the ultraviolet range.

Run on water
The common basilisk lizard, also known as Jesus Christ lizard, has the unique ability to run across water.

How the basilisk manages to pull off this incredible stunt is really due to physics. Adult basilisks tend to weigh around 200 grams (7 oz). The lizard uses its hind legs to propel itself across the water, usually reaching a maximum distance of 5 meters (15 ft) before beginning to sink.

Sleep with half of their brain
Wouldn't it be convenient never have to sleep? Well, if you were a cetacean, you could. Cetaceans are a group of marine mammals—consisting of dolphins, whales, orcas, and porpoises—that have the unique ability to sleep with one hemisphere of their brain at a time.

Have 360-degree vision
It's hard to imagine being able to see more than what we already can. However, for the chameleon, the human visual field is laughable. Chameleons are one of the two animals which are able to see in full 360-degree vision. The other animal is the dragonfly.

Based on: <https://listverse.com/2016/06/21/10-incredible-things-animals-can-do-that-we-cant/>.
Accessed on: Feb. 20, 2019.

a. ◯ Athletes abilities.
b. ◯ Human beings abilities.
c. ◯ Animals abilities.
d. ◯ Children abilities.

12 What is the best title for the article?
a. ◯ Animals and their bodies
b. ◯ Things animals can do that we can't
c. ◯ Where are these animals from?
d. ◯ Extinct animals and their abilities.
e. ◯ Abilities shared by animals and human beings.

13 Read the article again and write the name of the animal that matches each sentence.

a. It can see in full 360-degree vision. _____

b. It can run across water. _____

c. It can see colors that human beings can't. _____

d. It can sleep using only half of the brain. _____

14 Read the article once again and check **right**, **wrong** or **not mentioned**.
a. Birds' eyes are sensitive to the ultraviolet range.
   ◯ Right   ◯ Wrong   ◯ Not mentioned
b. A dolphin is a cetacean that floats while sleeping.
   ◯ Right   ◯ Wrong   ◯ Not mentioned
c. Birds have extra color cones in their retina.
   ◯ Right   ◯ Wrong   ◯ Not mentioned
d. A basilisk can reach a maximum distance of 15 meters before beginning to sink.
   ◯ Right   ◯ Wrong   ◯ Not mentioned
e. Chameleons are the only animals that can see in full 360-degree vision.
   ◯ Right   ◯ Wrong   ◯ Not mentioned

15 Which animal ability would you like to have? Why?

EXTRA PRACTICE

UNITS 7 AND 8

1 Read the timetable below. What kind of schedule is it presenting?

Summit Ridge Day Camp

Sample Week - Upper Camp

	MONDAY	TUESDAY	WEDNESDAY	THURSDAY	FRIDAY
8:50 - 9:15	←———————————— Meet and Greet ————————————→				
9:15 - 9:30	←———————————— Opening Circles ————————————→				
BLOCK 1 9:35 - 10:25	Computers	Archery	Karaoke/Music	Wacky Science	Field Games: Alaskan Baseball
BLOCK 2 10:25 - 11:15	Field Games: Capture the Flag	Wood Working	Ceramics	Epic Mini-golf	Archery
BLOCK 3 11:15 - 12:05	Cooking	Yoga Groove	Indoor Sports: Dodgeball	Hip-Hop	Make Your Own Music Video
BLOCK 4 12:05 - 12:55	LUNCH	LUNCH	LUNCH	LUNCH	LUNCH
BLOCK 5 12:55 - 1:45	Pool	FREE CHOICE	Pool	Waterslide & Games	FREE CHOICE
BLOCK 6 1:45 - 2:35	Ga-Ga		All Camp T-Sirt Tie Dye	Activity Center	
2:35 - 2:50	←———————————— Popsicle Time ————————————→				
2:50 - 3:15	←———————————— Closing Circle All Camp ————————————→				
3:15 - 3:45	←———————————— Dismissal #1 & #2 ————————————→				

Available at: <www.hendersonschool.com/student-life/summit-ridge-day-camp/activities-and-sample-schedule>.
Accessed on: Feb. 20, 2019.

a. ◯ It is a hiking camping schedule.

b. ◯ It is a canoe camping schedule.

c. ◯ It is a day camp schedule.

d. ◯ It is a day school schedule.

2 Read the timetable again and circle the correct answers.

a. The camping opens only on **weekdays/weekends**.
b. Activities are not offered in the **morning/evening**.
c. Free choice of activity is offered **everyday/some days of the week**.
d. Archery activity is offered **twice/three times** a week.
e. **Indoor/Outdoor** sports are practiced on Wednesdays.

3 Based on the timetable in activity 1, check the activities available in the camping.

a.
b.
c.
d.
e.
f.
g.
h.

4 Read the timetable once again and match the questions to the answers.

a. When is Meet and Greet?
b. What time does lunch break end?
c. How often are pool activities offered?
d. Is music activity offered every day?

○ No, it isn't.
○ Every morning.
○ Twice a week.
○ At twelve fifty-five.

5 Imagine you are the coordinator of a day camp. What activities would you offer in your camping?

ONE HUNDRED AND THIRTY-SEVEN 137

PROJECT 1
THE ENGLISH LANGUAGE

1 Many people speak English around the world. Check out the map below and find out which countries have English as a national, primary, or widely spoken language. After that, answer the following questions and discuss them with your teacher and classmates.

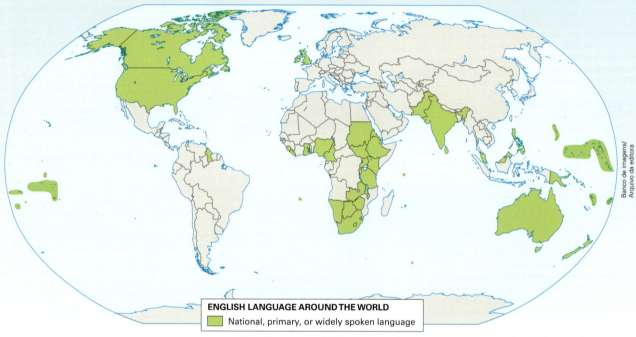

ENGLISH LANGUAGE AROUND THE WORLD
National, primary, or widely spoken language

Based on: <www.britannica.com/topic/English-language/media/188048/231155>.
Accessed on: Feb. 15, 2019.

a. What kind of map is it?
_____

b. Read the map captions and answer: what does the map highlight in green?
_____
_____

c. Do you recognize any of the countries in green? If so, which one(s)?
_____
_____

d. In your opinion, do people speak English only in the countries highlighted in green on the map? Why (not)?
_____
_____

2 Look at the chart below with your teacher and classmates. What kind of information is it showing?

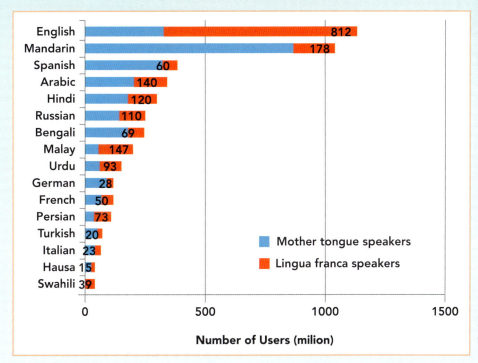

Available at: <https://chiasuanchong.com/tag/english-as-a-lingua-franca/>. Accessed on: Feb. 15, 2019.

3 Now you are going to discover how people speak English around the world. What accent do they have? Gather in groups, do some research, and present the results to your classmates.

PROJECT 2
BENEFITS OF PLAYING SPORTS

1 Read the infographic below. Then, discuss the questions with your teacher and classmates.

Available at: <https://believeperform.com/product/the-psychological-and-social-benefits-of-playing-sport/>. Accessed on: Feb. 26, 2019.

a. Which item of the infographic did you find more interesting? Why?

b. Do you think that playing sports brings benefits? If so, which one(s)?

c. Which sport has more psychological and social benefits to you? Explain your choice.

2 Now you are going to learn about three unusual sports that are practiced around the world. Are you ready?

Toe wrestling

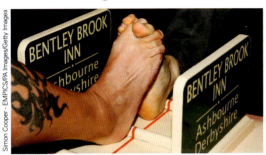

This sport is similar to arm wrestling, with players attempting to pin down their opponent's toes for about three seconds. Players play with their bare feet, alternating between their left and right feet, and play the best of three rounds. There are separate divisions for men and women. The World Toe Wrestling Championship has been ongoing since the 1970s and enjoys growing participation.

Underwater football

Underwater football is basically American football that's usually played in a swimming pool. Players have to wear snorkeling equipment and are tasked with getting the weighted football to the gutter on the other side of the pool.

Bubble soccer

In this quirky sport, players are strapped into huge inflatable bubbles, which cover their head and upper body. Each team typically consists of five players, and the game is played with much of the same rules that soccer has. This sport is not only incredibly fun to play but is also absolutely hilarious to watch!

Available at: <www.ba-bamail.com/content.aspx?emailid=15239>. Accessed on: Feb. 25, 2019.

> Assista a partes de uma competição de *toe wrestling* que ocorreu em Derbshyre, na Inglaterra. Disponível em: <https://www.youtube.com/watch?v=OjvMSS9ErSs>. Acesso em: 26 fev. 2019.

a. Underline in the text the words related to sports.

b. Which sport did you find more interesting? Why?

c. Look again at the infographic presented in activity 1 and read the text about the uncommon sports one more time. Do you think these unusual sports can be beneficial to life and health? Explain your answer.

3 Discover more about unusual sports that are practiced around the world. Gather in groups of three, do research, and present the results to your teacher and classmates.

FUN ACTIVITIES 1

1 Two e-pals are chatting online. Look at the image, unscramble the words, and complete the dialog.

Dayo: Hello! My name is Dayo. Good _____! (atrnofoen)

Juan: Hello, Dayo! My name is Juan. Nice to _____ you! (teme)

Dayo: Nice to meet you, too! I live in Lagos, the capital of _____. I'm Nigerian! (iagenNri)

Juan: Great! I live in Mexico City, the capital of Mexico. I'm _____! (xiencMa)

Dayo: Nice! What _____ is it in Mexico City? (itme)

Juan: It's noon. What time is in Nigeria now?

Dayo: It's _____ o'clock. (esnev)

2 In pairs, break the code and find out the hidden sentence about this family.

_____

_____

13 Look at the picture and label the rooms of the house. Then circle the name of the items you found inside the house.

| mirror | cabinets | microwave oven | table | sofa | telephone | desk |
| TV | fridge | stove | bed | toys | TV stand | bathtub |

14 Help Nina to go back to her hotel. Talk to a friend about which direction she needs to take to get there.

FUN ACTIVITIES 2

1 In pairs, read the sentences and find the animals to answer the riddles.

a. I am very big and lovable, but I can't be a pet because I am big, have big ears and a long trunk. Who am I?

_____

b. I can be small or I can be a big creature. I like to play and swing from a tree here to a tree there. I eat insects, flowers and fruit and I have a long tail. Sometimes I can be very naughty. Who am I?

_____

c. I am known as the king of the jungle. I have a big mane and I am very strong. I can scare people with my loud roar. Who am I?

_____

d. I have a long neck so I can eat leaves in tall trees. I am tall, tall and it's easy for me. Who am I?

_____

2 Find and circle eight words related to sports in the word search below.

F	B	E	X	E	R	C	I	S	E
C	O	U	R	T	H	A	A	G	P
L	D	I	B	X	Q	N	D	E	U
B	Y	A	Z	M	E	D	A	L	L
H	E	M	C	C	F	G	L	G	J
E	N	H	D	A	O	E	R	L	A
A	C	F	O	N	I	R	I	I	G
L	H	H	P	P	L	A	Y	E	R
T	E	A	M	M	E	A	S	H	X
H	E	S	D	G	O	A	L	Q	B
I	B	X	C	C	F	G	L	G	E

13 Complete the baskets with the name of the healthy foods you find in the box.

> apple   candies   cake   hamburger   carrot   papaya   pineapple
> orange   fish   grapes   tomato   onion   donuts   lettuce   tea
> nuts   egg   broccoli   eggplant

14 Find out what are today's plans for this family's summer vacation. Read the given example and complete the sentences and the crossword puzzle.

Have breakfast.   Go _____.   Have _____.   Go _____ on the lake.

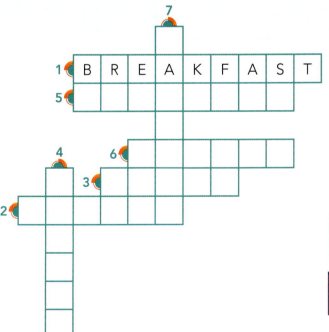

Go _____ at the beach.

Have _____.   Go _____.

GLOSSARY

abbey: abadia
ability: capacidade
able: ser capaz; hábil
about: a respeito de
above: acima de
absolutely: absolutamente, completamente
accent: sotaque
accepted: aceito/a
according to: de acordo com
achieve: alcançar
across: através de
act: agir; ato
action: ação
ad (advertisement): anúncio
added: adicionado/a
advantage: vantagem
after: após, depois de
after all: afinal de contas
afternoon: tarde
again: novamente
against: contra
age: idade
ago: atrás (tempo)
agree: concordar
ahead: à frente
aid: ajuda
air: ar
airport: aeroporto
alike: similar
all: todos/as; tudo
alligator: jacaré
all over: por toda a parte
all over the world: por todo o mundo
allow: permitir
along: por; ao longo de
a lot of: muitos/as
also: também
always: sempre
amazing: incrível
among: entre (várias coisas/pessoas)
amount: quantidade
angry: zangado/a
animation: animação (arte de animar desenhos e bonecos)

annoy: irritar
another: outro/a
ant: formiga
any: algum/a
appliance: eletrodoméstico
apply: aplicar
approaching: aproximando
arch: arco
archery: arco e flecha
arm: braço
around: ao redor de
as: como
Ash Wednesday: quarta-feira de cinzas
ask: perguntar; pedir
assistance: assistência, ajuda
assorted: variado/a
as well as: assim como
at: em; a
at all: em absoluto
aunt: tia
average: médio/a
avoid: evitar
away: distante

back: costas; atrás
backpack: mochila
backward: para trás
badminton: espécie de tênis jogado com raquete e peteca
bag: mala; sacola
bakery: padaria
ball: bola; baile
bare feet: pés descalços
based on: com base em
basket: cesta
bat: taco de beisebol
bathtub: banheira
be: ser; estar
beach: praia
beam: viga
bean: feijão
bear: urso
beat: batida, ritmo
because of: por causa de
because: porque (resposta)
bedroom: quarto

beet: beterraba
before: antes
began: começou
behind: atrás de
belief: crença
believe: acreditar, crer
bell: campainha, sino
bell pepper: pimentão
below: abaixo
benefit: beneficiar; benefício
berry: fruta silvestre
best: (o/a) melhor
better (than): melhor (que)
between: entre (duas coisas)
beverage: bebida
bind: unir
birdlike: parecido com um pássaro
birthday: aniversário
bite: morder; mordida
blank: lacuna; espaço em branco
blanket: cobertor
blind: cegar; cego/a
block: quarteirão
blueberry: mirtilo
board: lousa, quadro
boat: barco
boating: canoagem
body: corpo
bond: laço, elo
bone: osso
boost: aumentar
boot: bota
boring: chato/a
born: nascer; nascido/a
borrow: emprestar
both: ambos/ambas
bow: curvar-se; fazer reverência
bowl: tigela
box: caixa
brand name: marca
brand new: novo/a em folha
bread: pão
breath: respirar
breathe: respiração
brick: tijolo
bright: brilhante
bring: trazer
brother: irmão
brought: trouxe

brush: escovar; escova
bubble soccer: futebol na bolha
bucket: balde
bulletin board: quadro de aviso
bunch: maço
but: mas
buy: comprar
by: por

call: chamar; telefonar
calm: acalmar; calmo/a
came: veio
can: poder
candle: vela
caption: legenda
carefully: cuidadosamente
carrot: cenoura
cash: em dinheiro
catwalk: passarela
cauliflower: couve-flor
celebrate: comemorar
cetacean: cetáceo
challenge: desafiar; desafio
change: mudar, trocar; mudança
chant: canção rimada
character: personagem
charming: encantador/a
chart: quadro
cheap: barato/a
cheat: colar; trapacear
cheer: animar
cherry: cereja
chicken: frango
child: criança
children: crianças
chips: batata frita
choice: escolha
choose: escolher
chore: tarefa
church: igreja
clam: amêijoa (tipo de molusco)
classmate: colega de classe
classroom: sala de aula
clean: limpar; limpo
climb: escalar
clock: relógio
close to: perto de

146 ONE HUNDRED AND FORTY-SIX

closed: fechado/a
closest: mais próximo/a
cloud: nuvem
clown: palhaço/a
coach: treinar; treinador/a
coast: costa
coat: casaco
coin: moeda
cold: frio/a
collect: colecionar
college: faculdade
colorful: colorido/a
comb: pentear; pente
come: vir
comics: história em quadrinhos; tirinha
commonly: comumente
concerned: preocupado/a
cook: cozinhar; cozinheiro/a
cookie: biscoito, bolacha
cool: legal, bacana
corner: esquina
costume: fantasia
could: poderia
count: contar
country: país
court: quadra
courtyard: pátio
cousin: primo/a
cover: cobrir
crazy: maluco/a
create: criar
cross: atravessar
crowd: multidão
cruelty: crueldade
cry: chorar
currency: moeda corrente; dinheiro
current: atual
curtain: cortina
cushion: almofada
custom: costume
customer: cliente
cut: cortar; corte
cute: gracioso/a; bonito/a
cycling: ciclismo

dad: papai, pai
daily: diário/a; diariamente
dairy: laticínios
dark: escuro/a, escuridão
dear: querido/a
designer: desenhista, projetista
despite: apesar de
develop: desenvolver
device: artifício, dispositivo
died: morreu
dinette: espaço pequeno para refeições
dining room: sala de jantar
directions: instruções
dirt: sujeira
disability: incapacidade
disappear: desaparecer
discuss: discutir
disease: doença
dish: prato (refeição)
disposal: descarte
do: fazer
dolphin: golfinho
don't mind: não se importe
door: porta
doorbell: campainha
double: dobrar; duplo/a
down: abaixo
draft: rascunho
dragonfly: libélula
draw: desenhar
dream: sonhar; sonho
drink: beber
drive: dirigir
drugstore: farmácia
duck, duck, goose: variação do jogo pega-pega
duct tape: fita adesiva
during: durante
dust: tirar o pó; poeira, pó
duty: obrigação

each: cada
early: do/no início
earphones: fones de ouvido
easily: facilmente
Easter: Páscoa
eat: comer
egg: ovo
eighth: oitavo/a
eighteenth: décimo/a oitavo/a
eleventh: décimo/a primeiro/a
else: mais; outro/a
empower: empoderar
end: acabar; fim
endangered: ameaçado/a, em perigo de extinção
enemy: inimigo/a
engineering: engenharia
enjoy: divertir-se
enjoyment: diversão
enquiries: consultas, solicitações
entertainment: divertimento
environment: meio ambiente
environmental: ambiental
e-pal: amigo/a por correspondência pela internet
eraser: borracha
evening: noite
ever: sempre; alguma vez; já
every: todo/a
everybody: todos/as
everyone: todos/as
everything: tudo
excited: animado/a
exciting: empolgante
excuse: desculpar-se; desculpa
expensive: caro/a
expire: expirar, vencer

face: encarar; rosto
failure: falha
fair: justo/a
fair play: jogo justo
fake: fingir; falso/a
fall: cair; outono
famous: famoso/a
far: longe
farm: fazenda
fast: rápido/a
fat: gordo/a; gordura
Fat Tuesday: terça-feira gorda
father: pai
feat: feito, façanha
feather: pena
feature: característica
feeding: alimentando
feet: pés
female: mulher; fêmea
fence: cerca
fetch: trazer, buscar
field: campo
fifteenth: décimo/a quinto/a
fifth: quinto/a
fight: lutar; brigar; briga
file: arquivar; arquivo
fill in: preencher
find: achar
find out: descobrir
fine: ótimo/a, bem
finish: terminar
fireplace: lareira
first: primeiro/a
fisherman: pescador
fishing: pesca
fit: em forma
fitted: equipado/a
flag: bandeira
flag football: variação de jogo de futebol
flashlight: lanterna
flavor: sabor
floor: chão
floor plan: planta baixa
fluffy: fofo/a
flyer: folheto
folder: pasta
folks: pessoal, gente
follow: seguir
following: seguinte
for: por; para
forget: esquecer
forgot: esquecido/a
fourteenth: décimo/a quarto/a
fourth: quarto/a
free: livre
fresh: fresco/a
fridge: geladeira
fried: frito/a
friendly: amigavelmente
friendship: amizade
frisbee: jogo de arremesso de disco
frog: rã
from up there: de lá de cima
from: de (procedência)
front: frente
(in) front of: em frente ao/à
frozen: congelado/a
full: cheio/a
fun: diversão
funny: divertido/a, engraçado/a
furnishings: mobília
furniture: móvel, mobília

gap: abertura, lacuna
garbage bag: saco de lixo
garden: jardim
garlic: alho
gas station: posto de gasolina
gather: reunir(-se)
gender: gênero
general: geral
get: chegar; pegar; conseguir
get around: viajar para vários lugares
get off: sair (de um meio de transporte)
get together: estar junto, reunir-se
ghost: fantasma
gift: presente
ginger: gengibre
give: dar
given: dado/a
glad: contente
glittering: reluzente
glue: colar; cola
glue stick: cola bastão
go: ir
goal: meta
gonna: ir
good: bom/boa
go out: sair
gosh: caramba
grain: grão; cereais
grandfather: avô
grandmother: avó

grape: uva
grass: grama
great: ótimo/a; notável
greatness: grandeza
greenhouse: estufa
greeting: cumprimento
grocery: produtos alimentícios
ground: chão
grow: crescer
guess: adivinhar
gutter: calha; sarjeta
guy: rapaz
gym: academia

habitat: ambiente caracterizado por condições bióticas e abióticas; local onde alguém se sente em seu espaço ideal
hammock: rede de dormir
handsome: bonito
happen: acontecer
happy: feliz
has: tem
hat: chapéu
hate: odiar
haunted: mal-assombrado/a
have: ter
have fun: divertir-se
headquarter: sede; quartel-general
health: saúde
healthy: saudável
hear: ouvir
heart: coração
heaven: paraíso; céu
heavy: pesado/a
heel: salto
height: altura
help: ajudar; ajuda
hen: galinha
here: aqui
high: alto/a
highlight: destacar; destaque
highlighter: marca-texto
highway: autoestrada
hiking: fazer trilha
himself: ele mesmo
hind leg: pata traseira
hit: atingir; batida, golpe
hold: segurar; manter
holiday: feriado
home: lar
homegrown: cultivado/a domesticamente
honey: querido/a; mel
honour: honra
hope: esperar; esperança
house: casa
how: como

how often: com qual frequência
hug: abraçar; abraço
huge: enorme
humphead wrasse: napoleão (espécie de peixe)
hunt: caçar; caça
hurray: hurra

identify: identificar
if: se
ill: doente
improve: melhorar, incrementar
in: em; dentro de
in a hurry: apressado/a
in advance: com antecedência
include: incluir
increase: aumentar; aumento
incredibly: incrivelmente
indian: indígena
inflatable: inflável
injured: machucado/a
inside: a parte de dentro
instead of: em vez de, ao invés de
institution: instituição
interesting: interessante
intersection: cruzamento
interview: entrevistar; entrevista
into: para dentro de
introduce: introduzir; apresentar
invitation: convite
invite: convidar
island: ilha
issued: emitido/a
it doesn't matter: não importa

jellyfish: água-viva
join: juntar-se
judge: julgar; juiz/juíza
juggle: manipular, fazer malabarismos
juice: suco
jump: salto, pulo
junk: porcaria
just: apenas

keep: manter
keeper: responsável por
key: chave
kid: criança

kind: tipo; gentil
kindness: bondade
king: rei
kingdom: reino
kiss: beijo
kite: pipa
knife: faca
know: saber, conhecer

label: rótulo
lake: lago
land: pousar; terra
landmark: marco, ponto turístico
largest: maior
last: durar; último/a
late: atrasado/a
laugh: rir; risada
laughable: risível
laundromat: lavanderia automática
leadership: liderança
leaf: folha
leafy: folhoso/a
lean: sem gordura
learn: aprender
leave: deixar; ir embora
left: esquerdo/a
leisure: lazer
Lent: Quaresma
let: deixar
let's: vamos
letter: letra; carta
lie down: descansar
life: vida
lifespan: expectativa de vida
like: gostar; parecer; semelhante
list: listar; lista
listen: ouvir
litter: lixo
little: pequeno/a
live: viver
living room: sala de estar
lizard: lagarto
longer: por mais tempo; mais longo
look: olhar
look after: cuidar de alguém
look for: procurar
lost: perdido/a
low: baixo/a
low fat: baixo teor de gordura
lucky: sortudo/a
lyrics: letra de música

machine: máquina

main: principal
make: fazer
male: homem; macho (espécie animal)
mall: *shopping center*
manage: gerir; dar um jeito
mangrove: mangue
many: muitos/as
marbles: bolas de gude
marine: marinho/a
mark: assinalar
mask: máscara
match: relacionar
maybe: talvez
me: me, a mim
meal: refeição
mean: significar
mechanical pencil: lapiseira
meet: encontrar
memorable: inesquecível
mention: mencionar; menção
messaging: sistema de mensagem
microwave oven: forno de micro-ondas
midday: meio-dia
midnight: meia-noite
mile: milha
mind: mente
mindful: atento/a, cuidadoso/a
minus: menos
missing: ausente; perdido/a
mixed: variado/a
mom: mamãe
money: dinheiro
monkey: macaco/a
monster: monstro/a
month: mês
more: mais
most: mais; a maioria de
mother: mãe
mountain: montanha
move: movimentar; movimento
movie: filme
much: muito
muscle: músculo
must: dever (obrigação)
my: meu/minha

narrow: estreito/a
nature: natureza
near: perto
nearby: próximo/a
neck: pescoço
need: precisar; necessidade
net: rede
next: próximo/a
next to: ao lado de
nice: legal
nickname: apelido

nineteenth: décimo/a nono/a
ninth: nono/a
no longer: não mais
not: não
note: nota
notebook: caderno
noun: substantivo
now: agora
nowadays: atualmente
nuts: nozes

odd: estranho/a
of: de
offer: oferecer; oferta
offshoots: ramos
often: frequente
oils: gordura
on: em cima de, sobre
on its own: por si só
one legged: provido/a de uma só perna
only: somente
open: abrir
or: ou
ordinance: decreto, regulamento
other: outro/a
our: nosso/a
outside: fora, lado de fora
outstanding: excepcional
oven: forno
over here: por aqui
own: possuir; próprio/a

pack: empacotar; fazer a mala
paddle: remo
parade: desfile
pardon: perdão, desculpe
parking lot: estacionamento
particularly: especialmente
path: caminho
pay: pagar
pay attention: prestar atenção
peace: paz
peach: pêssego
pebbles: pedras miúdas
peel: descascar
pen: caneta
pencil: lápis
penny: centavo
pepper: pimenta
perhaps: talvez
person: pessoa
pet: animal de estimação
phone call: ligação telefônica
pick up: pegar; recolher

picture: pintura; foto
piece: pedaço
pillow: travesseiro
place: lugar
plan: planejar; plano
plate: prato
play: jogar; brincar
please: por favor
plenty: em abundância
plum: ameixa
plus: mais
pocket knife: canivete
poisonous: venenoso/a
polite: educado/a
pond: lagoa
pool: piscina
popcorn: pipoca
porch: varanda
porpoise: toninha (mamífero marinho)
possession: possessão
poster: cartaz
potato: batata
powder: pó
powerful: poderoso/a
prankster: brincalhão/brincalhona
prayer: oração, reza
prediction: previsão
pretty: bonito/a
prevention: prevenção
princess: princesa
procedure: procedimento
produce: produzir
projection: projeção
prop: suporte
propel: mover
provide: oferecer
publication: publicação
punishment: punição
purchase: comprar; compra
put: pôr

quarter: moeda estadunidense de 25 centavos; quarto de hora
queen: rainha
quick: rápido/a
quirky: peculiar

racing: corrida
radish: rabanete
rainbow: arco-íris
raincoat: capa de chuva
range: variação
rate: taxa
reach: alcançar; alcance
read: ler
ready: pronto/a
real estate: imóveis

really: realmente
reappear: reaparecer
reason: razão
rebuild: reconstruir
rebuilt: reconstruído/a
recall: recolher
referee: árbitro
refrain: refrão
related: relacionado/a
relatives: parentes
remain: ficar, permanecer
rent: alugar; aluguel
repair: consertar; conserto
replace: substituir; substituição
reply: responder; resposta
report: relatar; relatório
request: solicitar; solicitação
required: solicitado/a
research: pesquisar; pesquisa
resilience: resiliência
rest: descansar; descanso
restroom: banheiro, toalete
retime: fixar uma hora diferente; reprogramar
rewrite: reescrever
rhyming: que rima
rich: rico/a
ride: andar de; cavalgar
right: direito/a; correto/a
ring: tocar; som da campainha
ripe: maduro/a
ripen: amadurecer
river: rio
road: rua; estrada
roasted: assado/a
rock: pedra
room: sala; aposento
rooster: galo
root: raiz
rough: duro/a
round: redondo/a
rub: esfregar
rug: tapete
rule: regra
run: correr; corrida

sacred: sagrado/a
sad: triste
safety: seguro/a
same: mesmo/a
sample: amostra
sand: areia
saucy: atrevido/a
saved: salvo/a
say: dizer
scared: assustado/a
schedule: horário
school (of fish): cardume (de peixe)

schoolbag: mochila
score: placar, pontos
screen: tela
sculpture: escultura
sea: mar
search: procurar; busca
season: estação
second: segundo/a
see: ver
self-construction: construção feita pela própria pessoa
self-esteem: autoestima
sell: vender; venda
send: mandar, enviar
sent up: enviado/a
set: pôr; preparar; conjunto
set aside: reservar; reservado/a
set up: montar
seventeenth: décimo/a sétimo/a
seventh: sétimo/a
shake: sacudir, agitar
shake hands: dar as mãos
shanty: barraco
shape: formato
shared: compartilhado/a
shark: tubarão
sharpener: apontador
sheet: folha de papel
shining: brilhante
shoe: sapato
shoot: broto
shop: comprar; loja
shopping: compra
short: baixo/a, pequeno/a
should: dever
show: mostrar
show up: aparecer
shuttlecock: peteca
sibling: irmão/irmã
sign: assinar; placa, sinal
silly: bobo/a; estúpido/a
silver: prata; prateado/a
sin: pecado
since: desde
sing: cantar
sink: afundar; pia, lavabo
sir: senhor
sister: irmã
sit (down): sentar(-se)
sixteenth: décimo/a sexto/a
sixth: sexto/a
size: tamanho
skill: habilidade
skip: matar, cabular (aula)
sky: céu
sled/sledge: trenó
sleep: dormir
sleepy: sonolento/a
sleeve shirt: camisa de manga longa
slice: fatiar; fatia
slow: devagar

slum: favela, comunidade
smell: cheirar; cheiro
smile: sorrir; sorriso
snake: cobra
snow: neve
snowman: boneco de neve
so: então
soda: refrigerante
soft drink: bebida não alcoólica gaseificada
some: algum/a
something: alguma coisa, algo
song: canção
soon: logo
sorry: desculpe
south: sul
soy bean: soja
speak: falar
speed: velocidade
spell: soletrar
spend: gastar
spidergram: diagrama em forma de aranha
spinach: espinafre
spoken: falado/a
spoon: colher
spot: local, lugar; vaga
sprint: corrida de velocidade em distância curta
square meter: metro quadrado
stage: palco
stamina: resistência
stand (up): levantar(-se)
standing: estar em pé
starfish: estrela-do-mar
start: começar; começo
station: estação
stay: ficar; permanecer
strapped: afivelado/a
steamboat: barco a vapor
stick out: exibir; mostrar
still: ainda
sting: ferrão
stony corals: corais rochosos
stop: parar
store: loja
stove: fogão
straight: direto/a
strength: força
stressed vowel: vogal tônica
strike: soar, bater as horas
strip: tira
stripped: listrado/a
stroke: derrame
strong: forte
sunbathing: tomar sol
sunscreen: protetor solar
sunset: pôr do sol
supply: suprimento
support: apoiar; apoio
supportive: acolhedor/a; solidário/a

suppose: pressupor
sure: claro
surround: rodear
sweet: doce
sweetie: querido/a
swim: nadar
swimming: natação
swing: balançar
switch: virar; virada

tail: cauda
take: pegar; levar
take a look at: dar uma olhada em
take along: prolongar
take care: cuidar
take part: fazer parte
take place: acontecer
talk: falar
tall: alto/a
target: alvo
task: tarefa
teacher: professor/a
teenager: adolescente
tell: contar, dizer
tenth: décimo/a
than: do que
thank you: obrigado/a
that: aquele/a
theme: tema, assunto
themselves: eles/as mesmos/as
then: então
there: lá
these: estes/as
thin: magro/a
thing: coisa
think: achar, pensar
third: terceiro/a
thirteenth: décimo/a terceiro/a
this: este/a
those: aqueles/as
threaten: ameaçar
throw: atirar, jogar
tidy: asseado/a
time: tempo
timetable: cronograma
tip: dica
to: para
today: hoje
toe: dedo do pé
together: junto/a; juntos/as
tongue: língua
tongue twister: trava-língua
tonight: esta noite
too: também
took a trip: fez uma viagem
toothbrush: escova de dente
toothpaste: pasta de dente

top: topo, alto
torn: rasgado/a
tour: excursão; visita
tower: torre
town: cidade
toy: brinquedo
trace: rastro
train: trem
trap: enganar; armadilha
trash: lixo
travel: viajar
treated: tratado/a, cuidado/a
tree: árvore
tribe: tribo
trick on: pregar peças
true: verdadeiro/a
try: tentar
turn: virar
turtle: tartaruga
twelfth: décimo/a segundo/a
twentieth: vigésimo/a
twist: rebolar

ugly: feio/a
uncle: tio
uncountable: não contável
under: embaixo de
underline: sublinhar
understand: compreender
underwater football: futebol subaquático
unfortunately: infelizmente
unhappy: infeliz
united: unido/a
unity: união
unknown: desconhecido/a
unless: a menos que, a não ser que
unplug: desligado/a
unscramble: desembaralhar
until: até
up: para cima
useful: útil
usually: geralmente

V

vacation: férias
Valentine's day: Dia dos Namorados
values: valores
variety: variedade
vary: variar
very: muito
view: vista
village: vila
vines: videiras
voice: voz

voiced: sonoro/a

waist: cintura
wait: esperar
walk: andar
walking: caminhada
want: querer
watch: assistir; relógio
way: maneira; estilo
we: nós
weak: fraco/a
weapon: arma
wear: vestir
web: teia, rede
week: semana
weight: peso
weightlifting: halterofilismo
welcome: bem-vindo/a
well: bem
whale: baleia
what: o que; qual
wheelchair: cadeira de rodas
when: quando
where: onde
wherever: onde quer que
which: qual
while: enquanto
whistle: assobiar; apito
who: quem
whole: integral; completo/a
whom: de quem
whose: cujo/a
why: por que (pergunta)
wide: amplo
wild: selvagem
win: vencer
window: janela
wing: asa
winning: vencedor/a
wish: desejar; desejo
with: com
wolf: lobo
wonderful: maravilhoso/a
wood: madeira
word: palavra
work: trabalhar
world: mundo
wrestling: luta livre
write: escrever
wrong: errado/a

yard: quintal
year: ano
yell: gritar, berrar; grito, berro
young: jovem

GRAMMAR HELPER

UNIT 1

Subject Pronouns

Os *subject pronouns* são:

Singular					Plural		
I	You	He	She	It	We	You	They

1. O pronome *I* é sempre escrito com letra maiúscula.
2. Para se referir a um objeto ou animal, usa-se o pronome *it*. Para animais de estimação, por questões afetivas, geralmente são usados os pronomes *he* ou *she*.
3. O pronome *they* é usado para se referir tanto a pessoas como a animais e objetos no plural.

Verb to be – Simple Present

O verbo *to be* no presente do indicativo significa "ser" ou "estar". Em inglês, usa-se o mesmo verbo para designar esses dois sentidos.

O uso de formas contraídas (*contracted form* ou *short form*) é muito comum em conversação e também na escrita informal. Nas formas contraídas algumas letras são suprimidas e, em seu lugar, é colocado um apóstrofo ('), conforme mostram os exemplos a seguir.

I **am** happy. = I**'m** happy.

You **are** my best friend. = You**'re** my best friend.

She **is** an English teacher. = She**'s** an English teacher.

Subject Pronouns	Affirmative (Long form)	Affirmative (Contracted or short form)
I	am	'm
You	are	're
He/She/It	is	's
We/You/They	are	're

1 Complete the sentences with the correct form of the verb **to be**.

a. She _____ from Canada.

b. Elephants _____ very big animals.

c. I _____ fine, thank you.

d. The dog _____ brown.

UNIT 2

Verb to be – Negative form

Para criar frases na forma negativa do presente do indicativo, acrescenta-se a partícula *not* após o verbo *to be*. Leia os exemplos a seguir.

I am **not** at school.　　She is **not** in the kitchen.　　We are **not** Science teachers.

1 Complete the sentences using the negative form of the verb **to be**.

a. She _____ my mother.

b. We _____ late for school.

c. The cat _____ black and white.

d. My grandparents _____ from Japan.

Negative (Long form)	Negative (Contracted or short form)
I am not	I'm not
You are not	You aren't
He/She/It is not	He/She/It isn't
We/You/They are not	We/You/They aren't

Verb to be – Interrogative form

Para fazer perguntas usando o verbo *to be*, inverte-se a posição do verbo em relação à forma afirmativa, isto é, ele é colocado antes do sujeito. Veja o exemplo a seguir.

Affirmative form	Ms. Jones **is** my teacher.
Interrogative form	**Is** Ms. Jones my teacher?

2 Rewrite the sentences into the interrogative form.

a. She is English. _____

b. The boys are in the classroom now. _____

c. The band is ready to start the concert. _____

d. Jonas is in the bathroom. _____

Verb to be – Short answers

As respostas às perguntas feitas com o verbo *to be* são geralmente curtas – sem repetição da frase completa –, isto é, são compostas apenas de sujeito e de verbo auxiliar.

Observe, no quadro abaixo, que as contrações não são usadas na forma afirmativa.

	Affirmative	Negative
I	Yes, I **am**.	No, I**'m not**.
You	Yes, you **are**.	No, you **aren't**.
He/She/It	Yes, he/she/it **is**.	No, he/she/it **isn't**.
We/You/They	Yes, we/you/they **are**.	No, we/you/they **aren't**.

3 Answer the questions below. Use **short answers**.

a. Are you Brazilian? _____

b. Is the English teacher in the classroom? _____

c. Are your classmates working on their lessons? _____

Possessive Adjectives

Os adjetivos possessivos são posicionados antes do substantivo e indicam posse.

Subject Pronouns	Possessive Adjectives	Subject Pronouns	Possessive Adjectives
I	My	You	Your
I want to show you **my** soccer cards.		Hi, **uncle Bill**, is this **your** car?	
He	His	She	Her
He is my cousin Paul. **His** father is my uncle Bill.		**She** is my new English teacher. **Her** name is Sarah.	
It	Its	We	Our
This is a **race car**. **Its** motor is adapted for high speed circuits.		**We** need to study Geography. **Our** test is tomorrow.	
You	Your	They	Their
Are **you** back to **your** old school, kids?		**They** are English teachers and **their** parents are Math teachers.	

4 Complete the sentences with the correct possessive adjectives.

a. I love fruit juices. _____ favorites are lemon and orange juices.

b. John has a beautiful dog. _____ name is Goofy.

c. We are ready to start _____ lesson now, Ms. Montgomery.

d. Students, open _____ books to page 88, please.

Genitive Case

Para indicar posse, além de usar os adjetivos possessivos, pode-se usar o *genitive case*, acrescentando apóstrofo (') + s ('s) ao substantivo. Veja a seguir.

Whose computer is this?	It's Cinthia**'s**. It's **her** computer. It's Raphael and Sofia**'s**. It's **their** computer. It's the teacher**s'**. It's **their** computer.	**Whose** é o pronome interrogativo usado para perguntar a quem algo pertence.
Who is Pedro?	He's Henrique**'s** brother.	**Who** é o pronome interrogativo usado para perguntar quem é determinada pessoa.
Who are those people?	They're Gabriel**'s** classmates.	

1. Quando o substantivo termina em *s* ou está no plural irregular, acrescenta-se apenas o apóstrofo ('):

    This is the boy**s'** flashlight.   That is the teacher**s'** classroom.

2. Em caso de nomes próprios terminados em *s*, pode-se usar apenas o apóstrofo ou *'s*:

    This is the Browns**'s** trailer.   This is the Browns**'** trailer.

3. Observe nos exemplos que o caso genitivo é comumente utilizado quando o substantivo indica um ser animado (pessoas, animais, etc.). Em caso de seres inanimados e objetos, apenas usamos o genitivo para indicar posse nas seguintes exceções:

    a. Planeta Terra ou corpos celestes: *The Earth's route.*
    b. Grupo de pessoas: *The company's services.*
    c. Locais com nome de pessoas: *St. Patrick's Cathedral.*
    d. Medidas: *A kilo's weight of flour.*
    e. O "mundo": *The world's biggest statue.*
    f. Países: *Brazil's most famous sport is soccer.*
    g. Período de tempo: *In a month's time.*

5 Rewrite the sentences using **'s** to indicate possession.

  a. This pencil belongs to Caroline. _____

  b. This book belongs to my mother. _____

  c. This house belongs to David. _____

  d. This computer belongs to Gus. _____

UNIT 3

There to be

Usa-se a expressão *there to be* para indicar a existência de algo. Veja alguns exemplos no quadro a seguir.

	Affirmative	Interrogative	Negative
Singular	There is a sofa in the living room.	Is there a sofa in the living room?	There isn't (is not) a sofa in the living room.
Plural	There are two bedrooms in this house.	Are there two bedrooms in this house?	There aren't (are not) two bedrooms in this house.

1 Complete the following sentences using **there is** or **there are**.

  a. _____ 25 desks in my classroom.

  b. _____ one bathroom in the school.

  c. _____ 28 students in my classroom.

  d. _____ a notebook on my desk.

There to be – Short answers

Para responder a uma pergunta com *there to be*, usam-se as *short answers*, ou seja, a frase completa não é repetida.

	Affirmative	Negative
Singular	Yes, there **is**.	No, there **isn't** (**is not**).
Plural	Yes, there **are**.	No, there **aren't** (**are not**).

2 Answer the questions using some information about yourself and your school.

a. Are there two doors in your classroom? _____

b. Is there a Science book in your schoolbag? _____

c. Are there 80 chairs in your classroom? _____

d. Is there a blue pen in your pencil case? _____

UNIT 4

Prepositions of place

As preposições de lugar são usadas para indicar a posição de alguém ou de algo em relação a determinado espaço, ser ou objeto.

in   on   under   next to   in front of   behind   between   among

1 Underline the correct option from the prepositions in bold to complete the sentences.

a. The cat is **between**/**on** the sofa and the box.

b. Please, put your books **among**/**next to** your schoolbag.

c. Where is Katia? She's **under**/**in** the kitchen.

d. There is a notebook **among**/**in front of** the book.

Imperative

Os verbos no imperativo são usados para expressar uma ordem, uma instrução ou um pedido.

Na forma afirmativa, usamos o verbo no infinitivo, ou seja, sem o *to*. Na forma negativa, usamos *don't* no início da frase.

Affirmative	Negative
Go up.	**Don't turn** right.
Walk for five blocks.	**Don't park** the bus here.

2 Put the following words in the correct order to make sentences.

a. the exercise/the board/Copy/from _____

b. cell/Turn off/phone/your _____

c. talk/Don't/lesson/the/during/explanation _____

d. be late/Don't/your English test/for _____

UNIT 5

Articles

O artigo definido *the* é empregado antes de palavras masculinas e femininas, no singular ou no plural, e corresponde em português a "o", "a", "os", "as". Leia os exemplos a seguir.

The girl is at home.   **The** girls are at home.

Os artigos indefinidos *a* e *an* correspondem, ambos, a "um", "uma". São usados antes de substantivos no singular tanto no feminino como no masculino.

O artigo *a* é usado antes de consoantes ou palavras que começam com som de consoante:
a boy   **a** university

An é usado antes de vogais ou de palavras que começam com som de vogal:
an apple   **an** hour

1. Usa-se *an* antes de *h* mudo (**an** hour), mas usa-se *a* antes de *h* aspirado (**a** hospital, **a** house).
2. Usa-se *a* antes de *u* quando é pronunciado /yu/ (**a** university, **a** unit) e antes de *y* e *w* (**a** year, **a** wave).

1 Write **a** or **an**.

a. ____ bicycle   b. ____ old book   c. ____ pretty girl   d. ____ uniform   e. ____ hour

Can

Can é um verbo modal utilizado para expressar habilidade.

Nas frases afirmativas, *can* é usado entre o verbo e o sujeito.

Na forma interrogativa, inverte-se a ordem e *can* é posicionado antes do sujeito.

Na forma negativa, adiciona-se *not* ao modal, que, em sua forma contraída, fica *can't*.

Affirmative form	Monkeys **can** jump very high.
Interrogative	**Can** alligators swim?
Negative	Hippos **can't** breathe underwater.

2 Write sentences about yourself with the information offered. Use **can** or **can't**.

a. speak English: _____

b. run very fast: _____

c. eat vegetables every day: _____

UNIT 6

Present Continuous

O *Present Continuous* descreve uma ação que está em progresso, ou seja, que ainda está acontecendo no momento da fala. Na forma afirmativa, ele é formado pelo verbo *to be* mais o verbo principal terminado em *-ing*.

Affirmative	Subject	To be (Present)	Main verb ending in -ing
	Lisa	is	**studying** for a test.

Para frases na forma negativa, acrescenta-se *not* ao verbo *to be*. Também é possível usar a forma contraída.

Negative	Subject	To be (Present + not)	Main verb ending in -ing
	Lisa	is not (isn't)	**studying** for a test.

Para frases na forma interrogativa, inverte-se a ordem do verbo *to be* e do sujeito.

Interrogative	To be (Present)	Subject	Main verb ending in -ing
	Is	Lisa	**studying** for a test?

1 Complete the sentences with the verbs in the parentheses. Use the **Present Continuous**.

a. He _____ (do – negative) judo. He's hurt.

b. Your brother _____ (run – affirmative) now.

c. We _____ (play – affirmative) a soccer match.

d. They _____ (play – negative) beach volleyball today. It's raining.

Spelling rules for -ing form

Para obter verbos com a terminação *-ing*, é necessário observar certas regras:

para verbos regulares, adiciona-se *-ing* no final	Do	Do**ing**
para verbos terminados em *y*, adiciona-se apenas *-ing*	Play	Play**ing**
para verbos terminados em consoante + *e*, remove-se a letra *e* e adiciona-se *-ing*	Dance	Danc**ing**
para verbos terminados em *ee*, adiciona-se apenas *-ing*	See	See**ing**
para verbos terminados em consoante + vogal + consoante, dobra-se a última consoante e adiciona-se *-ing*	Sit	Sit**ting**

2 Write the verbs below with the **-ing** form.

a. plan _____

b. write _____

c. work _____

d. read _____

e. pay _____

f. cry _____

3 Now choose three verbs from activity 1. Then, in your notebook, write one affirmative, one negative and one interrogative sentence with each of the verbs.

Present Continuous – Short answers

Para responder de forma curta no *Present Continuous*, usa-se apenas o verbo *to be*.

Is she talking to her teacher?	Yes, she **is**./No, she **is not** (she **isn't**).
Are you playing online games?	Yes, I **am**./No, I **am not** (I'**m not**).
Are they playing soccer?	Yes, they **are**./No, they **are not** (they **aren't**).

4 Answer the following questions about you, your classroom and the weather.

a. Are the students doing the activity? _____

b. Is the teacher talking? _____

c. Are you paying attention? _____

d. Is it raining right now? _____

UNIT 7

Plural Forms

Para formar o plural da maior parte das palavras, acrescenta-se *s*.

+ s	apple – apple**s** onion – onion**s** pear – pear**s**

Nos substantivos terminados em consoantes + *y* (*ty*, *ly*, etc.), troca-se o *y* por *ies*.

y → ies	blueber**ry** – blueber**ries** cher**ry** – cher**ries** strawber**ry** – strawber**ries**

Aos substantivos terminados em *ch*, *sh*, *x*, *ss* e *o*, acrescenta-se *es*.

+ es	pea**ch** – pea**ches** radi**sh** – radi**shes** bo**x** – bo**xes** bo**ss** – bo**sses** potat**o** – potat**oes**

Em alguns substantivos terminados em *f* ou *fe*, troca-se *f*/*fe* por *ves*.

f/fe → ves	wol**f** – wol**ves** lea**f** – lea**ves** kni**fe** – kni**ves** li**fe** – li**ves**

Alguns substantivos têm o plural irregular, conforme mostrado a seguir.

child – children   man – men   woman – women   mouse – mice   foot – feet

1 What are the plural form of the words below? Write them down.

a. boy _____

b. apple _____

c. book _____

d. wife _____

e. family _____

f. kiss _____

Demonstrative Pronouns

O pronome demonstrativo *this* é usado para indicar pessoas, animais ou objetos próximos de quem fala. O plural de *this* é *these*.

This is my book.   →   **These** are my friends.

O pronome demonstrativo *that* é usado para indicar pessoas, animais ou objetos distantes de quem fala. O plural de *that* é *those*.

That car is big and red.   →   **Those** girls are having fun.

2 Choose the answers that complete the sentences appropriately.

a. _____ is my friend. Her name is Carla. (This/These)

b. _____ books over there are interesting. (That/Those)

c. _____ bike on the corner belongs to my father. (That/Those)

Simple Present – except the 3rd person singular

O *Simple Present* é usado quando se fala sobre o tempo presente, em geral, para se referir a ações que são um hábito ou que fazem parte da rotina.

Em frases afirmativas, usa-se o sujeito seguido do verbo e do predicado.

Affirmative	I/You/We/You/They	eat	vegetables and fruits every day.

Em sua forma negativa, usa-se o sujeito e o verbo auxiliar *don't* seguido do verbo e do predicado.

Negative	I/You/We/You/They	don't (do not)	eat	vegetables and fruits every day.

Em sua forma interrogativa, usa-se o verbo auxiliar *do* seguido do sujeito e do verbo com o predicado.

Interrogative	Do	I/You/We/You/They	eat	vegetables and fruits every day?

Para responder, usa-se a forma curta. Na forma afirmativa, usa-se *do* e na negativa, *don't*.

	Short answers	
Do they eat vegetables and fruit every day?	Affirmative form	Yes, they **do**.
	Negative form	No, they **don't**.

3 Put the words in the correct order and write sentences for each alternative.

a. English/study/every day/I _____

b. go/We/to the cinema/every Sunday _____

c. don't/I/have/homework today _____

d. listen/to music/They/every day _____

4 Answer the following questions about yourself.

a. Do you like to go to the beach? _____

b. Do you have any brothers or sisters? _____

c. Do your friends play video games? _____

UNIT 8

Simple Present – 3rd person singular

Affirmative form

Na forma afirmativa, quando usamos a terceira pessoa do singular (*he, she* ou *it*), em geral, adicionamos o *s* ao verbo.

Affirmative	He/She/It	drive**s**	to work.

No entanto, é importante estar atento às regras de escrita para a terceira pessoa do singular do presente simples:

na maior parte dos verbos, apenas acrescenta-se o *s*.	Buy Love	Buy**s** Love**s**
em verbos terminados em *s, z, x, o, sh* ou *ch*, adiciona-se *es*.	Do Kiss	Do**es** Kiss**es**
em verbos terminados em consoante + *y*, troca-se o *y* por *ies*.	Fly Study	Fl**ies** Stud**ies**

1 Write the 3rd person of the verbs in the parentheses.

a. She _____ (play) the piano and the guitar.

b. The teacher _____ (prepare) lessons at home.

c. My friend John _____ (watch) cartoons everyday.

Negative form

Na forma negativa, adiciona-se o *es* ao verbo auxiliar: *don't (do not)*, que se transforma em: *doesn't (does not)*.

Negative	He/She/It	do**esn't** (do**es** not)	drive to work.

2 Complete the sentences below according to the information in the parentheses.

a. Daniel _____ (like – affirmative) soccer very much.

b. She _____ (live – negative) near here.

c. Laura _____ (love – affirmative) rock music.

d. Lucas _____ (play – negative) basketball.

Interrogative form

Na forma interrogativa, acrescenta-se *es* ao verbo auxiliar *do*, transformando-o em *does*.

Interrogative	Does	he/she/it	drive to work?

Para responder, usam-se respostas curtas. Na resposta afirmativa, o auxiliar *do* vira *does*. Na resposta negativa, *don't* vira *doesn't*.

Short answers – 3rd person singular		
Does Amanda play the drums?	**Affirmative form**	Yes, she do**es**.
	Negative form	No, she do**esn't**.

3 Answer these questions about your teacher. Then check if you are right.

a. Does your teacher speak Italian? _____

b. Does your teacher like American football? _____

c. Does your teacher listen to classical music? _____

d. Does your teacher have a black car? _____

WORKBOOK

NAME: _____

CLASS: _____ DATE: _____

UNIT 1 – A GLOBAL WORLD

1 Read the dialog below and check the correct options to complete the sentences.

Annie: Hello, Michael. What are you doing?

Michael: I'm texting my friend, Ahunna.

Annie: Ahunna? Where is he from?

Michael: It's not a "he", it's a "she"! Ahunna is from Nigeria, she is Nigerian.

Annie: Wow! Where is Nigeria?

Michael: Oh, please, Annie! Don't you know where Nigeria is? It's in Africa!

Annie: I have a friend from another country too. Her name is Manar. She is from Syria.

Michael: Syria? Where is this country?

Annie: Oh, please, Michael! Don't you know where Syria is?

a. Michael and Annie have friends from _____.
   ○ the same country   ○ different countries

b. Ahunna's nationality is _____.
   ○ Nigerian   ○ Syrian

c. Manar is Annie's friend. She is from _____.
   ○ The USA   ○ Syria

2 Look at the pictures and complete the sentences with the countries and nationalities.

a.

Heidi is from _____.

She is _____.

b.

Raj is from _____.

He is _____.

c.

Anika is from _____.

She is _____.

d.

Rubén is from _____.

He is _____.

3 Complete the sentences with **is** or **are**. Then put them in order to create a meaningful text.

○ And he _____ a very good tennis player.

○ He _____ from Tokyo, Japan.

○ They _____ exchange students. They _____ best friends.

○ His friend Amanda _____ a good tennis player too. They play tennis after school every day.

① This is Makoto.

○ Amanda _____ not Japanese. She _____ Australian.

4 Check the picture that corresponds to Amanda and Makoto.

a.

b.

5 Unscramble the questions and answer them.

a. is/what/name/your/? _____

b. you/how/are/old/? _____

c. are/where/from/you/? _____

WORKBOOK

NAME: _____

CLASS: _____ DATE: _____

UNIT 2 – WHO IS THIS FAMILY?

1 Read the text and check the correct picture.

> Hi! I'm Jackson and this is my family. The name of my father is Joshua and he is my hero. My mom's name is Donna, she is a teacher. I have two sisters, Rachel and Lisa. Rachel is 12 years old and Lisa is a baby. I am 10 years old.

a.

b.

2 Look at the pictures and write one question for each image using the words given. Then answer them.

a.

Katy Perry/actress

b.

Adam Levine/band leader

c.

Lionel Messi and Gabriel Jesus/goalkeepers

_____   _____   _____

_____   _____   _____

_____   _____   _____

3 Imagine you are part of a celebrity family. Write a short text about it using the verb **to be** in the negative and affirmative forms. Answer the questions below to guide you.

- Who are your famous grandparents?
- Who are your famous parents?
- Do you have any famous brothers or sisters?
- What are their occupations?
- Why are they famous?

_____
_____
_____
_____
_____
_____
_____
_____
_____
_____
_____

4 Read and complete the dialog using the words from the box.

| 's (2x) | my | your | whose | it | you |

Mom: What a mess, Chris!

_____ sneakers are that?

Chris: They are Jackson _____, mom.

Mom: Is this _____ school bag?

Chris: No, _____ school bag is green.

_____ is Jackson _____ too, mom!

Mom: Jackson, _____ are in big trouble!

164 ONE HUNDRED AND SIXTY-FOUR

WORKBOOK

NAME: _____

CLASS: _____ DATE: _____

UNIT 3 – HOME SWEET HOME

1 Look at the picture, read the questions about it and answer them.

a. Is there a side by side refrigerator in the kitchen?

  _____

b. Are there any chairs?

  _____

c. Are there two sofas in the living room?

  _____

d. Are there two coffee tables?

  _____

e. Is there a rug in the living room? _____

f. Are there curtains in the living room? _____

2 Write questions using the words given and answer them according to what you can find at home.

a. a computer/your bedroom?

  _____

b. armchairs/the living room?

  _____

c. a microwave oven/the kitchen?

  _____

d. a double bed/your mom's bedroom?

  _____

3 Read the dialog and answer the questions.

Claudia: Hi, honey! Guess what? I found a furnished apartment for rent in Myrtle Beach! It's the perfect place for us to spend our vacation!

Tarik: Great news!

Claudia: There are three bedrooms and an open concept kitchen.

Tarik: How many bathrooms are there in the apartment?

Claudia: There are two bathrooms.

Tarik: Is there a dining room?

Claudia: No, there isn't. But there is a big table in the kitchen.

Tarik: Is it near the beach?

Claudia: Just two blocks away!

Tarik: Awesome!

a. Where is the apartment?

_____

b. How many bedrooms are there in the apartment?

_____

c. Is there a dining room?

_____

d. How far is the apartment from the beach?

_____

4 According to Claudia, the apartment in Myrtle Beach is furnished. Make a list of the furniture and home appliances you know/imagine that beach apartments have.

Bedroom: _____

Living room: _____

Kitchen: _____

Bathroom: _____

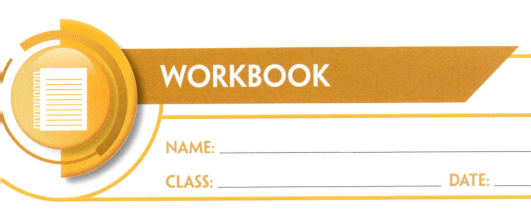

NAME: _____

CLASS: _____ DATE: _____

UNIT 4 – GETTING AROUND TOWN

1 Look at the city map and match the pictures to their corresponding names.

- ○ Internet cafe
- ○ movie theater
- ○ restaurant
- ○ bank
- ○ laundromat
- ○ bakery
- ○ gas station
- ○ bookstore
- ○ drugstore

2 Now, according to the map, underline the correct words to complete the sentences.

a. The Internet cafe is **among/in front of** the bank.

b. The bookstore is **behind/next to** the Internet cafe.

c. The bank is **between/in front of** the movie theater and the bakery.

d. The bakery is **under/across from** the restaurant.

3 What do the signs below stand for? Check the correct answers.

a.

○ Turn right.
○ Turn left.

b.

○ Park your car here.
○ Don't park.

c.

○ Don't turn right.
○ Don't stop.

d.

○ Don't walk here.
○ Don't drive here.

4 Complete the chart with the affirmative and negative forms of the imperative sentences.

Imperative – Affirmative	Imperative – Negative
	Don't walk one block.
	Don't bring your pets.
Go straight ahead.	
Turn left.	

WORKBOOK

NAME: _____

CLASS: _____ DATE: _____

UNIT 5 – ANIMAL WORLD

1 Look at the pictures and complete the sentences with the name of the animals.

The fingerprints of a _____ are so indistinguishable from the human ones that they have on occasion been confused at a crime scene.

_____ are the only animals that can't jump.

A _____'s horn is made of hair.

A _____ gives nearly 200 000 glasses of milk in a lifetime.

_____ have no vocal chords.

An _____'s eye is bigger than its brain.

Based on: <www.thedodo.com/16-amazing-animal-facts-1094218100.html>. Accessed on: Feb. 18, 2019.

2 What are these animals capable of doing? Check the correct answers.

	Ostrich	Cow	Elephant	Koala
Can jump				
Can swim				
Can run fast				
Can sleep in a tree				

3 Read the text and write the names according to their descriptions.

> This picture shows some of my friends. The tall boy is Matt and the short girl next to him is his sister Amelia. She is so young, but she is the best student in school. The one with the dog is me, Louis. The thin man next to me is Mr. Thorn, Matt's grandfather and he can do some amazing magic tricks. He is the best magician in the world!

WORKBOOK

NAME: _____

CLASS: _____ DATE: _____

UNIT 6 – I CAN PLAY BASKETBALL

1 Look at the pictures and match them to their corresponding sports. There are some extra sports mentioned.

- ◯ athletics
- ◯ badminton
- ◯ canoeing
- ◯ judo
- ◯ tennis
- ◯ volleyball
- ◯ basketball
- ◯ swimming
- ◯ soccer

2 Who is your favorite athlete? Do some research and write about him/her.

_____
_____
_____
_____
_____
_____
_____
_____
_____
_____
_____
_____

3   Write questions and answers using the Present Continuous. Follow the example.

a. Chloe/play/basketball
   no/play/video game
   Is Chloe playing basketball?
   No, she isn't. She is playing video game.

b. Tessa/study Math
   no/rest
   _____
   _____

c. the Winthorps/watch/sports on TV
   no/play/soccer
   _____
   _____

d. Carlo and Paolo/swim
   yes
   _____
   _____

4   Look at the pictures and name the people according to activity 3.

_____

_____

_____

_____

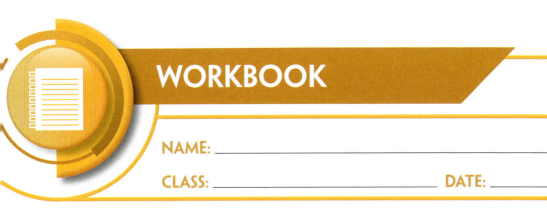

WORKBOOK

NAME: _____

CLASS: _____ DATE: _____

UNIT 7 – YOU ARE WHAT YOU EAT

1 Use the words from the box to complete the dialog.

| countries | England | euro | hamburgers |
| junk food | money | pound | vegetables |

Sophie: Hey, Dan! You are from _____, aren't you?

Dan: Yes, I'm from Cambridge. Why?

Sophie: I'm going to Europe and I would like to know how much _____ I will need for buying food there.

Dan: Which _____ are you going to visit?

Sophie: England, Portugal and Spain.

Dan: Well, it depends on the country. The currency in Portugal and Spain is _____,

which is a little cheaper than the _____ from England.

Sophie: OK! What about the price of food there?

Dan: In those countries you can have cheap _____, such as

_____ and fries, pizza, soda etc. But if you prefer healthy food,

like _____, fruit, fish or chicken, I can give you a list of my favorite restaurants. Some of them are more expensive, some of them aren't. It's your choice!

Sophie: Wow, thank you, Dan!

2 Imagine you are Sophie's friend. Talk about your favorite healthy food restaurant. Send her a message and share what you usually eat and how much money you spent there.

_____
_____
_____
_____

3 Read the sentences and underline the mistakes. Then rewrite them in the correct form.

a.

Look at all that vegetables in the basket! Three carrot, some potato and one big eggplants. I'm hungry!

_____
_____

b.

Does you see that woman over there? She is my cousin and these are her childs.

_____
_____

4 Read the text and answer the questions.

The Currencies of The European Nations

Currently, 28 currencies are used by the fifty European nations, with the Euro being the most popularly used currency.

Currency is an important object in the exchange of goods and services around the world. Currencies include banknotes and coins [...].

Available at: <www.worldatlas.com/articles/the-currencies-of-the-european-nations.html>. Accessed on: Feb. 19, 2019.

a. Do Europeans use only one currency in the continent?

_____

b. Do currencies include only banknotes?

_____

c. What is the most popular currency in Europe?

_____

WORKBOOK

NAME: _____

CLASS: _____ DATE: _____

UNIT 8 – LET'S GO CAMPING!

1 Read the text below and answer the questions using full answers.

Jack

Hi, Michael. How's it going? I have a surprise for you. Tina and I are going camping with some friends! 😳 Would you like to join us? Tina has all the equipment and we enjoy cooking! She is an expert in hamburgers and I'm in baked potatoes. Our friend Jason is in charge of fishing. He fishes very well.

Mandy, Tina's sister, loves roasting marshmallows and I play the guitar at night. It's so much fun! 😜 Also, we can swim in the lake. Except Tina, she doesn't like to swim. So, would you like to come?

a. Does Mandy have all the equipment to go camping?
_____

b. Does Jason fish well?
_____

c. Does Tina love roasting marshmallows?
_____

d. Who plays the guitar?
_____

e. Does Tina like to swim?
_____

2 Look at the pictures and check the items needed for camping. Then write their names.

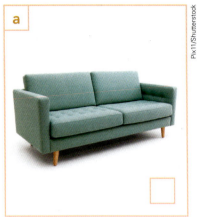 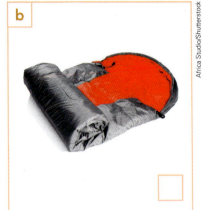 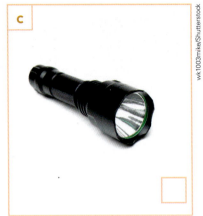

_____   _____   _____

_____   _____   _____

3 Follow the example and write sentences in the Simple Present tense.

a. Bob/clean the camping site every day (affirmative sentence)
   Bob cleans the camping site every day.

b. The Millers/go camping every summer (interrogative sentence)
   _____

c. My father/fix anything (negative sentence)
   _____

d. Ann/go hiking with her friends every morning (affirmative sentence)
   _____

e. Jill and Rachel/go horseback riding (negative sentence)
   _____

Direção Presidência: Mario Ghio Júnior
Direção de Conteúdo e Operações: Wilson Troque
Direção editorial: Luiz Tonolli e Lidiane Vivaldini Olo
Gestão de projeto editorial: Mirian Senra
Gestão de área: Alice Silvestre
Coordenação: Renato Malkov
Edição: Ana Lucia Militello, Carla Fernanda Nascimento (assist.), Caroline Santos, Danuza Dias Gonçalves, Maiza Prande Bernardello, Milena Rocha (assist.), Sabrina Cairo Bileski
Planejamento e controle de produção: Patrícia Eiras e Adjane Queiroz
Revisão: Hélia de Jesus Gonsaga (ger.), Kátia Scaff Marques (coord.), Rosângela Muricy (coord.), Ana Paula C. Malfa, Brenda T. M. Morais, Diego Carbone, Gabriela M. Andrade; Amanda T. Silva e Bárbara de M. Genereze (estagiárias)
Arte: Daniela Amaral (ger.), Catherine Saori Ishihara (coord.) e Letícia Lavôr (edit. arte)
Iconografia e tratamento de imagem: Sílvio Kligin (ger.), Claudia Bertolazzi (coord.), Carlos Luvizari (pesquisa iconográfica), Cesar Wolf e Fernanda Crevin (tratamento)
Licenciamento de conteúdos de terceiros: Thiago Fontana (coord.), Flavia Zambon e Angra Marques (licenciamento de textos), Erika Ramires, Luciana Pedrosa Bierbauer, Luciana Cardoso Sousa e Claudia Rodrigues (analistas adm.)
Ilustrações: Igor RAS
Cartografia: Eric Fuzii (coord.), Robson Rosendo da Rocha (edit. arte)
Design: Gláucia Koller (ger.), Talita Guedes (proj. gráfico e capa), Luis Vassallo (capa) e Gustavo Vanini (assist. arte)
Foto de capa: vitormarigo/Shutterstock e David Neil Madden/Moment/Getty Images

Todos os direitos reservados por Editora Ática S.A.
Avenida das Nações Unidas, 7221, 3º andar, Setor A
Pinheiros – São Paulo – SP – CEP 05425-902
Tel.: 4003-3061
www.atica.com.br / editora@atica.com.br

2023
Código da obra CL 742202
CAE 648308 (AL) / 648309 (PR)
8ª edição
5ª impressão
De acordo com a BNCC.

Impressão e acabamento: EGB Editora Gráfica Bernardi Ltda.

#DAY1

PIAUÍ, BRAZIL

At Customs

Tina: Well, people, this is day one of my video log and I decided to show you my arrival in Piauí, Brazil!

Customs officer: Good afternoon. Your passport, please.

Tina: Here it is.

Customs officer: What's your name?

Tina: I'm Tina Traveler.

Customs officer: How long are you planning to stay?

Tina: About two weeks.

Customs officer: Business or pleasure?

Tina: Pleasure. I really want to visit Serra da Capivara National Park.

Customs officer: OK! Here is your passport.

Tina: Thank you, sir.

Customs officer: You're welcome, young lady.

 Brazil
Capital: Brasília, DF
Location: South America
Area: 8,515,767 sq. km
Population: 211,912,707
Currency: Real
Official language: Portuguese
Nationality: Brazilian

Piauí

CROSS CULTURAL

> Serra da Capivara National Park is a Unesco World Heritage Site. It is famous for its cave paintings. Some of them are more than 25,000 years old.

1 Complete the sentences.

a. The colors of Brazil's flag are _____, _____, _____ and _____.

b. Serra da Capivara National Park is in Piauí, Brazil. It is famous for its _____.

2 Fill in the blanks with the words from the box.

| is (2×)   I'm   are   my |

Tina Around the World
Published in January 15

SUBSCRIBE

Follow me while I travel the world. Now, _____ in Brazil to visit Serra da Capivara National Park, in Piauí. The park _____ amazing! Animals _____ everywhere, and the vegetation _____ just incredible. But the most beautiful things in the park are the cave paintings, in _____ opinion. Don't forget to subscribe. Love, Tina.

3 Choose the correct answer from the box and fill in the blanks.

| Hello!   You're welcome.   No, I'm a tourist guide.
My name is José Silveira.   Yes, I am. I'm Brazilian. |

Interview with a Serra da Capivara National Park's tourist guide.

Tina: Hello!

Guide: _____

Tina: What's your name?

Guide: _____

Tina: Are you a tourist here?

Guide: _____

Tina: Are you from Brazil?

Guide: _____

Tina: OK, success for you and thanks for the interview.

Guide: _____

5

#DAY42

GEORGETOWN, GUYANA

Checking in at the Hostel

Tina: Hi! I have a reservation for a four-bedded room with a bath.

Receptionist: Hello and welcome to our hostel! Name, please?

Tina: I'm Tina.

Receptionist: OK, Tina. Let me just check your reservation. Here it is. There is an air conditioning in every room and we have laundry service, too. Breakfast is served from 7 to 10 a.m. We hope you enjoy your stay!

Tina: What place do you recommend a visit here in Georgetown?

Receptionist: I strongly recommend you take a walk on Main Street. It is a great way to get to know the city.

Tina: Great! My next video will be there! Thanks a lot.

Receptionist: No problem. Your room is 606. Here is your key. Welcome to Georgetown!

CROSS CULTURAL

English is Guyana's official language, but most of the population speak Guyanese Creole as their native tongue. English is the language used for education, government, media, and services.

1 Answer the questions.

a. What is the official language in Guyana? Is it also Guyanese people's native tongue?
_____

b. What is the official language in your country?
_____

2 Match the places to their meanings.

a. room service   ◯ the place to wash clothes
b. laundry room   ◯ the place where people are greeted
c. reception room   ◯ the hotel serves food, drinks etc. in your room

3 Underline the correct answers according to the dialog.

a. Breakfast starts at **7/10** a.m.
b. There **is/isn't** a bath in Tina's room.
c. Tina is staying in a **hotel/hostel**.
d. The receptionist recommends the **City/Main Street**.

Guyana
Capital: Georgetown
Location: South America
Area: 214,970 sq. km
Population: 740,685
Currency: Guyanese dollar
Official language: English
Nationality: Guyanese

PORT OF SPAIN, TRINIDAD AND TOBAGO

#DAY60

Taking a Taxi

Tina: Excuse me, sir?

Porter: Yes.

Tina: Where are the taxis?

Porter: The taxis are over there.

Tina: Please, can you take my bags to the taxi?

Porter: Sure. It's three dollars, miss.

Tina: Here it is. Thanks a lot! By the way, are you Trinidadian?

Porter: Yes, I am.

Tina: This island is really beautiful!

Porter: Thank you!

Trinidad and Tobago
Capital: Port of Spain
Location: Central America
Area: 5,131 sq. km
Population: 1,374,408
Currency: Trinidadian dollar
Official language: English
Nationalities: Trinidadian, Tobagonian

CROSS CULTURAL

Trinidad and Tobago are two separate islands. The first European to reach them was Christopher Columbus. The island's present name comes from the word tobacco. Calypso, a popular folk Caribbean music, is from Trinidad.

1 Match.

a. The first European to reach the islands.   ◯ Tobacco.
b. The name Tobago comes from this word.   ◯ Calypso.
c. A popular folk Caribbean music.   ◯ Columbus.

2 Underline the correct word according to the dialog.

a. There is a **bus/taxi** stop near Tina.
b. Tina paid three dollars to the **porter/taxi driver**.
c. The porter was born in **Trinidad/Tobago**.

3 Look at the map of Tobago and do the following:

a. Circle 3 beaches where it is possible to bath.
b. Write the name of 3 beauty spots.

_____

c. Make an X on 3 spots of snorkel/diving.
d. How many historical sites are there in Tobago?

_____

#DAY81
KINGSTON, JAMAICA

Meeting Local People

Tina: Hi, I'm Tina.
Ziggy: Hello, Tina. I'm Ziggy. Where are you from?
Tina: I'm from San Francisco.
Ziggy: Oh, California. A sunny place, too.
Tina: Yes. What's this?
Ziggy: It's my bongo. I play it every day.
Tina: Nice, can you play it now?
Ziggy: Sure. Do you like music?
Tina: I do! I love music.
Ziggy: I play reggae music.

🇯🇲 Jamaica
Capital: Kingston
Location: Central America
Area: 10,992 sq. km
Population: 2,904,039
Currency: Jamaican dollar
Official language: English
Nationality: Jamaican

CROSS CULTURAL

> Reggae is a type of popular music from Jamaica and a national symbol. The most famous reggae singer is Bob Marley.

1 Complete the sentences.

a. The colors of Jamaica's flag are _____, _____ and _____.

b. Reggae is a _____ of Jamaica.

2 Fill in the blanks with the words from the box.

| are | beautiful |
| our | I'm | is |

Hi, Mom, Dad and Jennifer

Everything _____ great in Jamaica. _____ having a lot of fun.

The people _____ very friendly.

There are so many _____ beaches here! I miss you all a lot. I'm taking so many pictures! Jennifer, don't forget to feed _____ turtle.

Bye for now.
Love, Tina

Mom and Dad Traveler
2828 Wentworth Rd.
San Francisco
U.S.A.

3 Choose the correct answer from the box and fill in the blanks.

| You're welcome. | Yes, I am. I'm Jamaican. |
| My name's Jimmy Marley. | Hello! | No, I'm a reggae singer. |

Interview with a reggae singer

Tina: Hello!

Singer: _____

Tina: What's your name?

Singer: _____

Tina: Are you a pop singer?

Singer: _____

Tina: Are you from Jamaica?

Singer: _____

Tina: OK, success for you and thanks for the interview.

Singer: _____

#DAY117

SAN JUAN, PUERTO RICO

Tina is Hungry

Tina: Excuse me, can I have the menu, please?

Waiter: Yes. Here it is. Anything to drink?

Tina: Yes, an orange juice, please.

Waiter: What about a starter?

Tina: A salad, please.

Waiter: And for the main course?

Tina: Sweet and sour chicken.

Waiter: OK, *pollo agridulce*. What about some *arroz con dulce* for dessert?

Tina: Pardon?

Waiter: Some sweet rice pudding.

Tina: Oh, OK. I'll try it.

Waiter: Good! I'll be right back, miss.

Puerto Rico

Capital: San Juan
Location: Central America
Area: 9,104 sq. km
Population: 3,195,153
Currency: American dollar
Official languages: Spanish, English
Nationality: Puerto Rican

Salsa is a typical vibrant and dynamic Puerto Rican dance music. It blends sounds of various musical genres and is famous around the world.

1 Underline the correct word according to the text.

a. **Salsa/Samba** is the most influential form of music from **Jamaica/Puerto Rico**.

b. Salsa is **heard/despised** all over the world.

c. Salsa refers to the **calm and sweet/vibrant and dynamic** Puerto Rican **song/dance**.

2 Choose an image to answer the following questions.

a. Who is talking to Tina?

b. What is she having for lunch?

c. What is she having for dessert?

3 Read the Puerto Rican Tostones recipe. Then complete with the words from the box.

| oil | sprinkle | slices | peel | fry |

Ingredients:
- 2 green plantains
- 2 cups of vegetable oil

Procedure:

_____ the plantains and cut them in _____. Place the pieces in salt water. In a deep frying pan, heat the oil. Add the plantain slices to the hot _____ and _____ them until they turn a light golden color. Drain them on paper towels, _____ with salt and serve them hot. You can put ketchup or mojito (garlic, olive oil and salt mixture) on them, if desired. Enjoy!

Based on: <www.elcolmadito.com/USRecetasDetailEnglish.asp?Numero=67>. Accessed on: Apr. 5, 2019.

#DAY203

NASSAU, THE BAHAMAS

A Very Good Trip

Ted: Traveling by ship is marvelous!

Tina: I really like it, but sometimes it can turn into a bad experience.

Ted: Why?

Tina: Because of the bad weather. In the Caribbean Islands, people can get sick.

Ted: Really?

Tina: Yeah! The ship moves a lot more when the weather is bad. And people get seasick. Sometimes they stay in their cabin the whole time!

Ted: So, I guess we're lucky!

Tina: Definitely! The days are sunny and the sea is calm.

Ted: But don't forget that having a good partner is also important! Ha, ha, ha…

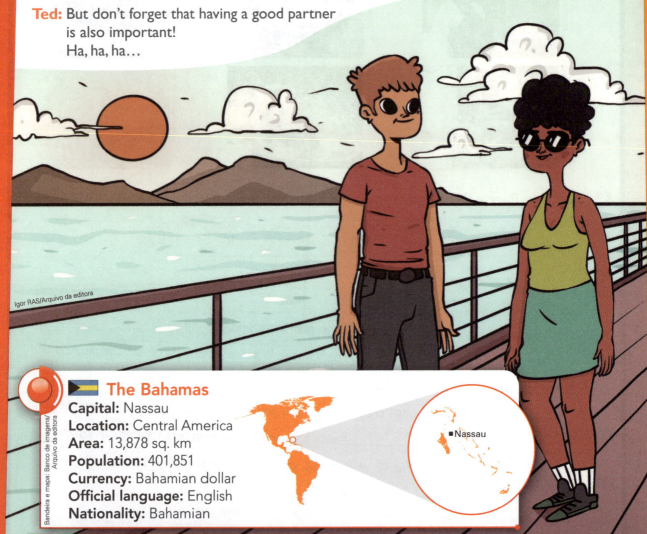

The Bahamas
Capital: Nassau
Location: Central America
Area: 13,878 sq. km
Population: 401,851
Currency: Bahamian dollar
Official language: English
Nationality: Bahamian

> In 1492, Christopher Columbus made his first landfall in the New World on the San Salvador island, in the Bahamas. After observing the shallow sea around the islands, he said "baja mar" (shallow water or sea), and named the area The Bahamas or The Islands of the Shallow Sea.

1 Answer the questions.

   a. Where did Columbus first land in the New World, in 1492?

      _____
      _____

   b. Why do the islands have the *Bahamas* name?

      _____
      _____

2 Underline the correct word according to the text.

   a. Tina and Ted are in **Nassau/Caribbean/Iceland**, in the Bahamas.

   b. Tina explains that people can feel **well/deceived/sick** in a ship in the Caribbean Islands.

   c. Tina says that the sea is **good/calm/ship**.

   d. Ted thinks that a good **trip/ship/partner** is important, too.

3 Answer the questions according to the text in the card.

> **If you like the outdoors and nature, you are invited to a meeting with the Ship's Underwater Specialist for a presentation of the Bahamas.**
>
> The meeting will offer information about beautiful beaches, snorkeling, underwater marine life and equipment rental.
>
> **TIME:** 2:30 P.M.
> **VENUE:** BLUE SAPPHIRE LOUNGE LOCATED ON ATLANTIC & PROMENADE DECKS FORWARD.
>
> **CASUAL CLOTHES ARE REQUIRED!**

   a. What? _____

   b. Where? _____

   c. When? _____

   d. What kind of clothes should people wear? _____

NEW YORK CITY, THE UNITED STATES OF AMERICA

At the Theater

Tina: Excuse me. What time is it, please?

Camila: Oh, sorry! I don't have a watch.

Tina: That's OK… You have a different accent. Where are you from?

Camila: I'm from Brazil. What's your name?

Tina: My name is Tina.

Camila: I'm Camila. Nice to meet you, Tina.

Tina: Nice to meet you, too. Is this your first time in New York?

Camila: Yes, it is. Oh! The play is going to start. Enjoy it!

 **The United States of America**
Capital: Washington, D.C.
Location: North America
Area: 9,833,517 sq. km
Population: 328,530,143
Currency: American dollar
Language: English
Nationality: American

 New York

THE STATUE OF LIBERTY, NEW YORK CITY.

When people arrive in the harbor of New York by ship, they are welcomed by the Statue of Liberty. The "Lady with the Torch" was given to the U.S. by the French government.

1 Answer the questions.

a. Does the Statue of Liberty have another name?

_____

b. Is there any important statue in your city? Which one?

_____

2 Rewrite the sentences following the example.

a. Camila is from Brazil.

She is Brazilian.

b. Tina is from the U.S.

_____

c. Tina has a friend who is from Japan.

_____

3 Fill in the blanks with the words from the box.

| missing | know | show | hope | tomorrow |

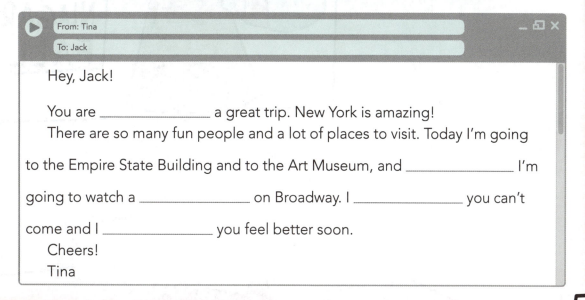

From: Tina
To: Jack

Hey, Jack!

You are _____ a great trip. New York is amazing! There are so many fun people and a lot of places to visit. Today I'm going to the Empire State Building and to the Art Museum, and _____ I'm going to watch a _____ on Broadway. I _____ you can't come and I _____ you feel better soon.

Cheers!
Tina

17

TORONTO, CANADA

A Day Tour

Attendant: Good morning. How can I help you?

Tina: I would like to go on a tour to Niagara Falls. How much is it?

Attendant: It's 150 Canadian dollars. Should I make you a reservation?

Tina: Yes, please.

Attendant: What's your name and where are you staying?

Tina: My name is Tina Traveler. I'm at the Downtown Hotel.

Attendant: Our bus will pick you up at the hotel at 8 a.m. Please, wait in the lobby. Our guide will call you by your name. Here is your ticket.

Tina: Can I pay now?

Attendant: Sure. Thanks!

Tina: Thank you.

Canada
Capital: Ottawa
Location: North America
Area: 9,984,670 sq. km
Population: 35,121,728
Currency: Canadian dollar
Languages: English and French
Nationality: Canadian

CROSS CULTURAL

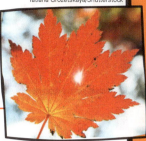

English and French are the two Canadian official languages. Approximately 85% of the population speaks one or the other.
The maple leaf and the beavers are important national symbols.

1 Correct the information in the sentences.

   a. The tour costs 120 Canadian dollars.
   _____

   b. The bus will pick Tina up at the hotel room.
   _____

   c. Tina wants to go to the hotel.
   _____

2 Underline the correct word according to the text.

   a. Tina is staying in a **hotel/hostel**.
   b. Tina is going to wake up **late/early**.
   c. Tina has a **card/ticket**.
   d. The attendant offers Tina a **reservation/bus**.

3 Read the folder and answer the questions.

   a. Where is Niagara Falls?
   _____

   b. How much per cent can you save according to the folder?
   _____

   c. Which are the four top Niagara Fall's attractions?
   _____
   _____
   _____
   _____

LET'S LEARN MORE ABOUT AMERICA

America is divided into three regions: North America, South America, and Central America.

The name is derived from the Italian explorer Amerigo Vespucci, who made several voyages to the Western Hemisphere and described them in letters to friends in Italy.

Amerigo Vespucci was friends with Christopher Columbus, who traveled to parts of America, as the Bahamas, Cuba, Santo Domingo and Jamaica. Later, he traveled the coasts of eastern Central America and north South America.

As there are many countries in America, there are also many languages as Spanish, Portuguese, English, French, Dutch and various native indigenous languages.

Based on: <https://www.dictionary.com/e/usa-names/>. Accessed on: Apr. 8, 2019.

America has a variety of natural beauties and everywhere you go there is something different to see. Here are some of them:

YELLOWKNIFE, CANADA
SEE THE NORTHERN LIGHTS IN CANADA'S NORTHWEST TERRITORIES CAPITAL.

ALASKA, USA
VISIT MORE THAN 13 MILES OF ICY CAVES.

SAN PEDRO DE ATACAMA, CHILE
COME AND SPEND SOME TIME IN THIS COOL ARID REGION THAT STRETCHES TO THE BORDER OF PERU.

PANTANAL, BRAZIL
BETWEEN MATO GROSSO AND MATO GROSSO DO SUL, IT HAS AN IMPRESSIVE BIODIVERSITY.

BUENOS AIRES, ARGENTINA
AMERICA IS NOT ONLY ABOUT OUTDOOR EXUBERANCE. VISIT EL ATENEO. ORIGINALLY A GRAND THEATER, THEN A GRAND CINEMA AND NOW ONE OF THE BIGGEST BOOKSTORES IN THE WORLD.

What about you? Search on-line for the best places to visit in America. Start your own bucket list.

BRAZIL

FERNANDO DE NORONHA

PORCOS BAY AND MORRO DOIS IRMÃOS, FERNANDO DE NORONHA, PERNAMBUCO, BRAZIL.

Fernando de Noronha is an isolated group of volcanic islands in the South Atlantic, approximately 215 miles from the state of Rio Grande do Norte and 340 miles from Pernambuco.

The main islands are the visible parts of a range of submerged mountains. The base of this enormous volcanic formation is 2,480 feet below the surface.

The Archipelago Fernando de Noronha hosts ecologic sites ideal for marine life, due to its geographic location, as well as the nature of its climate.

In 1988, approximately 70% of the archipelago was declared a National Marine Park, with the goal of preserving land and marine environment. It is administered by Ibama. Towards its goal, research projects are being developed, such as: recording native and migratory bird species both marine and land; shark research and the Tamar Project (marine turtles).

Permanent works built by the NGOs and foundations contribute to the perfecting of the conservational policies.

Based on: <www.pbase.com/marciocabral/noronha_island>. Accessed on: Mar. 13, 2019.

1 Answer the questions.

a. Where is Fernando de Noronha?
___
___

b. What is the name of the institute that administers Fernando de Noronha?
___

c. What is the name of the project to protect marine turtles?
___

d. Why is the archipelago a National Marine Park?
___
___

e. Who helps to preserve Fernando de Noronha?
___

GUYANA

KAIETEUR FALLS

KAIETEUR FALLS, GUYANA.

    Guyana is a small country, bordered by Brazil, Suriname and Venezuela. It has emerged as the playground for explorers that want to go in an adventure in its beaches in the north, mountains in the west and rainforests and savannahs in the south. You choose, Guyana has it all.

    One of the country's natural wonders is the majestic Kaieteur Falls. It is almost five times as tall as Niagara Falls, in Canada. It is considered to be one of the most powerful single drop waterfalls in the world, with 741 feet.

    When you visit this number 2 rated in the World's Top 100 Highest Rated Waterfalls, you start with an aerial view, as the aircraft circles over the Falls and the National Park before it lands.

    Most people that visit Guyana say the Falls leave you awestruck and it is the highlight of the trip.

Based on: <www.guyanatourism.com/natural-wonders/#waterfalls>. Accessed on: Mar. 13, 2019.

1 Underline the correct option.

   a. Kaieteur Falls is rated number **three/two** in the World's Top Highest Falls.

   b. Guyana is bordered by **three/two** different countries.

   c. The Kaieteur Falls is in **Canada/the National Park**.

   d. People can visit **beaches/bays** in Guyana.

2 Write **T** (true) or **F** (false).

   a. ◯ There are rainforests and savannahs in Guyana.

   b. ◯ The mountains can be found in the east.

   c. ◯ Kaieteur Falls is the highlight of a trip to Guyana for most people.

TRINIDAD AND TOBAGO

SCARBOROUGH

Officially, the Republic of Trinidad and Tobago is a twin island country in the Caribbean. After being colony of different nations, they were ceded to Britain in 1802 as separate states, but then were unified in 1889. The islands became independent and a republic in 1976.

The capital city is Port of Spain, located in Trinidad. But Scarborough is the second largest city and it is located in Tobago.

One of the main points of interest and history in Tobago is the Fort King George, built between 1777 and 1779 by the British.

From the top, that is 450 feet above the sea, the Fort offers a panoramic view of Scarborough, the south part of Tobago, the east coast and the central hills.

Based on: <https://www.discovertnt.com/articles/Tobago/Tobago-Capital-Scarborough/179/4/9#axzz5h82bglGJ>. Accessed on: Mar. 13, 2019.

LIGHTHOUSE AT FORT KING GEORGE, TOBAGO.

1 Complete the sentences with words from the box.

> city　　feet　　British　　island

a. The fort is 450 _____ above the sea.

b. Trinidad and Tobago is a twin _____ in the Caribbean.

c. Scarborough is the second largest _____.

d. Fort King George was built by the _____.

2 Answer the questions.

a. What is the capital city of Trinidad?

_____

b. Where can you have a panoramic view of Scarborough?

_____

JAMAICA

SAINT ANN'S BAY

SAINT ANN'S BAY, OCHO RIOS, JAMAICA.

When Christopher Columbus arrived in Jamaica, in 1494, he anchored at Saint Ann's Bay. He found the first inhabitants, the Arwaks, and slaved them to farm sugar and tobacco.

As they soon died because of the bad living conditions, the Spanish imported African slaves to work in Jamaica.

Even when the British captured the island, they continued to import slaves. But in 1739, the Maroons, who were runaway slaves, fought with the British and gained independence to live in the hills. The total independence came only in 1962.

Once a place that received enslaved people from Africa, today, Saint Ann's Bay is a neighborhood with beautiful beaches and that receives tourists. It's near several locations to learn more about the history of Jamaica.

Based on: <https://jis.gov.jm/information/jamaican-history/>. Accessed on: Mar. 13, 2019.

1 What happened in these years?

a. 1494

_____

b. 1962

_____

2 Circle the correct answer.

a. The Spanish imported **African**/**Arwaks** slaves.

b. The Maroons were **British**/**runaway** slaves.

c. Christopher Columbus arrived in **Jamaica**/**Africa**.

PUERTO RICO

ISLA DE VIEQUES

ISLA DE VIEQUES, PUERTO RICO.

    This is a small island and home to the largest natural wildlife refuge in the Caribbean, located seven miles off the east coast of Puerto Rico. It's one of the few destinations that remains like the Caribbean of the past: quiet, uncrowded and with unmatched natural beauty.

    There are no traffic lights, the narrow roads lead to awesome spots, and the beaches are free of development.

    Going to the southern shore of the island, there's the bioluminescent bay, called Mosquito Bay. It has been declared the brightest recorded in the world! It's a magical natural wonder and it's best experienced during the new moon.

    In the waters of the bay there are organisms that, when in contact with another organism or when are shaken, produce a bright burst of blue light. Just spectacular.

Based on: <https://vieques.com/>; <https://vieques.com/island-bioluminescent-bay/>. Accessed on: Mar. 13, 2019.

1 Answer the questions.

    a. Where is Isla de Vieques located?

    _____

    b. Are there traffic lights in the island?

    _____

    c. What is the name of the bioluminescent bay?

    _____

    d. What happens when the organisms in the water are in contact with another organism?

    _____

2 What words can describe Isla de Vieques? Circle them in the text.

THE BAHAMAS

NASSAU

Nassau is located on the 21-mile-long island of New Providence and is connected, via bridge, to Paradise Island, another popular Bahamian destination. Nassau, with its blend of influences from West Africa to England and from Haiti to the United States, is one of the most popular (and often congested) cruise ports in the Caribbean and the Bahamas.

The city of Nassau is warm, and has sunny climate, resort facilities including gambling casinos, a range of duty-free shopping stops, a large harbor, and historic landmarks, such as the two 18th century forts. It has soft, white soft-sanded beaches and friendly people.

The city, settled in the mid-1600s, became an administrative center in 1671 and was heavily fortified in the 18th century to provide protection from the numerous attacks by the Spanish and by pirates.

Based on: <http://www.bahamas-travel.info/nassau.htm>. Accessed on: Mar. 13, 2019.

NASSAU, THE BAHAMAS.

Stefan Ugljevarevic/Shutterstock

1 Write **T** (true) or **F** (false).

a. ◯ Paradise Island is a Bahamian popular destination.

b. ◯ Nassau is located in Paradise Island.

c. ◯ There are two forts in Nassau.

d. ◯ Pirates attacked Nassau in the 18th century.

2 Complete the sentences with information from the text.

a. Nassau is one of the most popular _____ ports in the Caribbean.

b. Nassau has soft, white soft-sanded _____ and friendly _____.

THE UNITED STATES OF AMERICA

GRAND CANYON

GRAND CANYON NATIONAL PARK, ARIZONA, U.S.

The United States offer many touristic attractions. One of them is the Grand Canyon National Park, in the state of Arizona. It is considered one of the Seven Natural Wonders of the World.

It was formed by erosion, and its layers are a spectacular feature. From the top of the rims, when you see a tiny ribbon, that's the Colorado River.

Today, there are three major rims that attract tourists, but the South and North Rims are the most popular.

The South Rim never closes and is the most accessible, with over 5 million visitors per year. The North Rim doesn't offer many services, it is very remote and is closed in the winter. However, people believe that the views are more incredible than the ones in the South.

Based on: <https://www.arizona-leisure.com/grand-canyon-history.html>. Accessed on: Mar. 13, 2019.

1 Answer the questions.

a. Where is the Grand Canyon National Park?

_____

b. What can you see from the top of the rim?

_____

c. Which are the most popular rims?

_____

d. How many people visit the South Rim every year?

_____

e. In which rim can you have the most beautiful views?

_____

CANADA

WHISTLER

Just two hours north of Vancouver, in British Columbia, you can find Whistler. This is Canada's favorite destination, no matter when you're visiting it. There are two mountains to be explored, Whistler and Blackcomb, with a vibrant base village. There, you can find accommodations that suits every budget, as well as hiking trails, spas and the best mountain bike park in the world. It is a popular destination for snow lovers and adventurous people that like skiing.

On February 14, 1966, Whistler Mountain opened for skiers. The resort made several bids to host an Olympic Games, but it wasn't until 2010 that it was finally selected as host. The 2010 Olympic and Paralympic Winter Games left memorable moments in the life of the inhabitants of the area.

Based on: <https://www.whistler.com/about-whistler/olympics/>. Accessed on: Mar. 13, 2019.

ALTA LAKE, WHISTLER, BRITISH COLUMBIA, CANADA.

1 Complete the sentences with words from the box.

| accommodations | skiers | Columbia | mountains |

a. Whistler is located in British _____.

b. Whistler and Blackcomb are two _____.

c. You can find different kinds of _____.

d. Whistler mountain opened for _____ in 1966.

2 Underline the correct option.

a. Whistler was selected to be the host of the Olympic Games in **1966/2010**.

b. The Games left **memorable/terrible** moments in the life of the inhabitants.

c. The mountains are located two hours north of **Vancouver/Canada**.

29

GLOSSARY

above: acima
accent: sotaque
accessible: acessível
accommodation: acomodação
according: de acordo
add: adicionar
administer: administrar
adventure: aventura
adventurous: aventureiro
aerial: aéreo
African: africano
after: depois
air conditioning: ar-condicionado
aircraft: aeronave
almost: quase
amazing: incrível
American: americano
anchor: ancorar
another: outro
anything: algo
approximately: aproximadamente
archipelago: arquipélago
arid: árido
around: ao redor
arrival: chegada
arrive: chegar
Atlantic: Atlântico
attack: atacar
attendant: atendente
attraction: atração
awesome: impressionante
awestruck: impressionado

bag: mala
Bahamian: bahamense
bath: banho
bathing: tomar banho
bay: baía
beach: praia
beautiful: bonito
beauty: beleza
beaver: castor
because: porque
become: tornar

before: antes
believe: acreditar
below: abaixo
(the) best: o melhor
better: melhor
between: entre
biggest: o maior
biodiversity: biodiversidade
bioluminescent: bioluminescente
bird: pássaro
black: preto
blank: em branco
blend: misturar
bongo: bongô
bookstore: livraria
border: fronteira
bordered: no limite
both: ambos
box: caixa
Brazilian: brasileiro
breakfast: café da manhã
bridge: ponte
brightest: mais brilhante
bring: trazer
British: britânico
bucket list: lista do que fazer antes de morrer
budget: orçamento
build: construir
bus: ônibus

cabin: cabine
calm: calmo
can: poder
capture: capturar
card: cartão
Caribbean: caribenho
carry: carregar
cave: caverna
cede: ceder
century: século
check in: fazer o *check-in*
chicken: galinha
choose: escolher
circle: circular
city: cidade
climate: clima
clothes: roupa
coast: costa

colony: colônia
come: vir
congested: congestionado
connect: conectar
conservational: de conservação
consider: considerar
continent: continente
contribute: contribuir
cool: legal
cost: custar
country: país
create: criar
cross cultural: envolver duas ou mais culturas, ideias e costumes
cruise: cruzeiro
Cuban: cubano
cup: xícara
currency: moeda corrente
customs: alfândega
cut: cortar

dad: papai
dance: dançar
day: dia
deceive: enganar/iludir
decide: decidir
deck: convés
declare: declarar
deep: fundo
definitely: definitivamente
derive: derivar
describe: descrever
desire: desejar
dessert: sobremesa
destination: destino
develop: desenvolver
development: desenvolvimento
die: morrer
divide: dividir
diving: mergulho
dollar: dólar
doubt: dúvida
downtown: centro da cidade
drain: drenar
drink: beber; bebida

drop: queda
due: esperado
duty-free: livre de impostos
dynamic: dinâmico

early: cedo
east: leste
eastern: do leste
ecologic: ecológico
education: educação
emerge: emergir
enjoy: desfrutar/curtir
enormous: enorme
environment: meio ambiente
episode: episódio
erosion: erosão
European: europeu
even: até mesmo
everything: tudo
everywhere: em toda parte
excuse me: com licença
experience: experiência
explain: explicar
explore: explorar
explorer: explorador
exuberance: exuberância

facility: instalação
famous: famoso
farm: cultivar
favorite: favorito
feature: característica
feed: alimentar
feel: sentir
feet: pés
few: pouco
find: encontrar
first: primeiro
flag: bandeira
folder: pasta
folk: folclórico
follow: seguir
following: o seguinte

forget: esquecer
formation: formação
fort: forte
forward: adiante
foundation: fundação
four: quatro
four-bedded: com quatro camas
French: francês
friend: amigo
friendly: amigável
from: de
fry: fritar
frying pan: frigideira
full: cheio
fun: divertido

gain: ganhar
gambling: apostar/jogar
garlic: alho
genre: gênero
get sick: ficar doente
goal: objetivo
golden: dourado
government: governo
great: ótimo
green: verde
guess: supor
guide: guia
Guyanese: guianês

harbor: porto
have: ter
hear: ouvir
heat: aquecer
heavily: bem/muito
help: ajudar
here: aqui
highest: mais alto
highlight: destaque
hiking: caminhada
hill: colina
historical: histórico
home: lar
hope: esperar
host: recepcionar/hospedar
hostel: hospedaria
hot: quente

how long: quanto tempo
how much: quanto
however: entretanto
hungry: com fome

icy: gelado
import: importar
important: importante
impressive: impressionante
including: incluindo
incredible: incrível
independent: independente
influence: influência
information: informação
ingredient: ingrediente
inhabitant: habitante
interest: interesse
interview: entrevista
invite: convidar
island: ilha
isolated: isolado

Jamaican: jamaicano
Japanese: japonês
job: trabalho
juice: suco
just: simplesmente

keep: manter
key: chave
kind: tipo
know: conhecer/saber

lady: senhora
land: aterrissar/pousar
language: idioma
large: grande
largest: maior
late: tarde
laundry: lavanderia
layer: camada
lead: conduzir

leaf: folha
learn: aprender
letter: carta
life: vida
light: luz
like: gostar; como
live: viver
lobby: saguão
located: localizado
location: localização
love: amar
lucky: com sorte
lunch: almoço

main: principal
main course: prato principal
majestic: majestoso
major: principal
make: fazer
many: muitos
maple: bordo
marine: marinho
marvelous: maravilhoso
match: combinar
matter: assunto
media: mídia
meet: encontrar
meeting: reunião/encontro
memorable: memorável
menu: cardápio
migratory: migratório
mile: milha
miss: sentir falta
mixture: mistura
mom: mamãe
moon: lua
move: mudar
museum: museu
music: música

narrow: estreito
nation: nação
national: nacional
nationality: nacionalidade
native: nativo
nature: natureza
near: perto

neighborhood: vizinhança
next: próximo
nice: agradável/simpático
north: norte
now: agora
numerous: numeroso

observe: observar
offer: oferecer
officer: oficial/funcionário
official: oficial
officially: oficialmente
often: frequentemente
oil: óleo
olive: azeitona
one: um
opinion: opinião
orange: laranja
organism: organismo
outdoor: ao ar livre
over: sobre
own: próprio

painting: pintura
panoramic: panorâmico
paper towel: papel-toalha
pardon: desculpe
parents: pais
park: parque
partner: sócio/parceiro
passport: passaporte
pay: pagar
peel: descascar
people: pessoas
per cent: por cento
perfect: aperfeiçoar
permanent: permanente
pick (someone) up: buscar
piece: pedaço
pirate: pirata
place: colocar; lugar
plan: planejar
play: jogar/tocar; peça teatral
pleasure: prazer
policy: política
population: população
porter: carregador (de malas)

powerful: poderoso
presentation: apresentação
preserve: preservar
procedure: procedimento
project: projeto
protection: proteção
provide: providenciar
pudding: pudim
Puerto Rican: porto-riquenho

quiet: quieto

rainforest: floresta tropical
range: extensão/alcance
rate: avaliar
reach: alcançar
really: realmente
receive: receber
receptionist: recepcionista
recipe: receita
recommend: recomendar
recommendation: recomendação
record: gravar
refer: referir
region: região
remain: permanecer
remote: remoto
rental: aluguel
republic: república
require: requer
research: pesquisar
reservation: reserva
resort: estância/balneário
rhythm: ritmo
ribbon: fita
rice: arroz
rim: borda
river: rio
road: estrada
room: quarto/sala
runaway: escapar

safety: segurança
salad: salada
salt: sal

savannah: savana/planície
save: economizar
say: dizer
sea: mar
seasick: estar enjoado
see: ver
sentence: sentença
separate: separar
serve: servir
service: serviço
set: molho (de chaves)
settle: instalar-se/estabelecer-se
seven: sete
several: muitos
shake: sacudir
shallow: raso
share: compartilhar
shark: tubarão
ship: navio
shore: orla
should: deveria
show: mostrar
sick: doente
singer: cantor
single: único
sir: senhor
site: sítio/local/*site*
ski: esquiar
skier: esquiador
slave: escravo; escravizar
slice: fatiar
snorkel: tudo de respiração
snorkeling: mergulho
snow: neve
soft: suave
soft-sanded: de areia macia
something: alguma coisa
song: canção
soon: breve
sour: azedo
southern: do sul
Spanish: espanhol
speak: falar
specie: espécie
spend: gastar
spot: lugar
sprinkle: salpicar
start: começar
starter: entrada
state: estado
statue: estátua
stay: hospedar-se
stretch: entender-se

strongly: fortemente
submerge: submergir
subscribe: inscrever-se
success: sucesso
such as: tal como
sugar: açúcar
suit: cair bem (roupa)
sunny: ensolarado
sure: certamente
surface: superfície
sweet: doce
symbol: símbolo

take picture: tirar foto
talk: falar
terrible: terrível
text: texto
theater: teatro
there: lá
think: pensar
three: três
ticket: tíquete
time: hora/tempo
tobacco: tabaco
Tobagonian: relativo a Tobago
today: hoje
tomorrow: amanhã
tongue: língua
tour: excursão
tourist: turista
tourist guide: guia turístico
towards: em direção a
traffic light: semáforo
trail: trilha
travel: viajar
traveler: viajante
Trinidadian: relativo a Trinidad
trip: viagem
turn: vez
turtle: tartaruga
twin: gêmeo
two: dois
type: tipo

uncrowd: não aglomerado
under: embaixo de
underline: sublinhar

unified: unificado
unmatched: inigualável
until: até

variety: variedade
various: vários
vegetable: vegetal
vegetation: vegetação
venue: local
vibrant: vibrante
view: vista
village: aldeia
visible: visível
volcanic: vulcânico
voyage: viagem

waiter: garçom
wake up: acordar
walk: andar
waltz: valsa
want: querer
warm: quente
wash: lavar
watch: assistir; relógio de pulso
water: água
waterfall: cachoeira
weather: clima
welcome: bem-vindo
well: bem
west: oeste
western: a oeste/ocidental
what: o que
where: onde
while: enquanto
white: branco
who: quem
whole: todo
why: por que
wildlife: fauna
winter: inverno
wonder: admiração
world: mundo

years old: anos de idade
yellow: amarelo
young: jovem